Manifestes
6

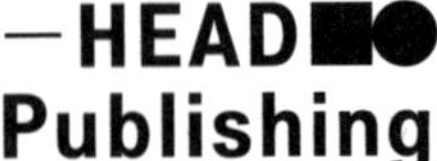
—HEAD Publishing

Philippe Rahm
The Anthropocene Style

Before the 20th century, interior decoration in the Western world served various practical functions: to ward off the cold in winter, to enhance the faint light seeping in through small windows set in thick, heavy walls and to block the draughts blowing in around all the windows and doors, bringing cold air that set the inhabitants' teeth achatter. Back in the day, rugs were laid on the floor to keep one's feet warm and tapestries hung up to insulate the walls and keep the heat in. Crystal chandeliers, along with mirrors and gilded decorations, reflected and refracted the faint light emanating from candles and windows, thereby brightening the room. A folding screen (*paravent* in French) served to 'block the wind' *(parer le vent)*—i.e., to deflect the cold air of convection currents from bare skin. And curtains served to block draughts, to smother them in their thick wool and prevent them from carrying off the meagre heat produced by burning a few logs of scarce and costly wood in the fireplace.

Interior decoration's initially utilitarian, climate-regulating function was rendered obsolete and superfluous by the advent of modern building technologies in the early 20th century, namely central heating, electric lighting and air conditioning, all of which were powered by the combustion of hydrocarbons. Thanks to massive use of fossil fuels (coal, natural gas and oil), modern technologies proved far more effective at improving thermal comfort—supplying domestic warmth and cooling, as well as artificial light—on an scale unprecedented in human history. One had only to open the radiator valve to release a steady flow of heat wholly unknown to human habitations prior to the 20th century. At the flick of a switch, interiors could be lit up so brightly at night as to simulate broad daylight. People could now take down all the tapestries and curtains, roll up the rugs and fold up the screens that had so faithfully, if somewhat ineffectually, staved off the cold for untold centuries, and put away the candlesticks that had produced such feeble light. All these hallowed decorative devices promptly gave way to the bare white interiors characteristic of the 20th-century modernity championed by Le Corbusier and his contemporaries—an aesthetic predicated on the release of CO_2 from oil-burning boilers and coal-burning power plants.

In its fossil-fuel-induced stupor, the 20th century then gradually forgot what interior decoration was for in the first place. Having lost sight of its practical, thermal, physiological purpose, Western society eventually came to the conclusion that it was of no real use—except to lay claim to a certain social standing or classist prestige, a symbolic distinction based on the rarity, beauty, costliness and opulence of one's chandeliers, tapestries, curtains, mirrors and gilded decorations and fittings.

But all that has changed since 1990. This modernist illusion has been shattered by heat waves that now make some interiors uninhabitable in summer, by the return of chilly indoor temperatures in winter due to rising energy bills, and by the urgent need to reduce CO_2 emissions from our buildings in order to limit global warming. These climate hazards reveal the true cost of doing away with the old decorative devices: our modern comforts and austere modern aesthetic are contingent on an all-out dependence on fossil fuels. The fight to curb global warming is currently ushering in a transition from 20th-century minimalism, which is now outmoded, to a new utilitarian and fashionable 21st-century decorative style that we call 'the Anthropocene style'. Its object is to reduce household energy consumption and CO_2 emissions whilst passively improving thermal comfort in the winter and in scorching summers.

At the interface of architecture, aesthetics and engineering, this book is a manifesto for a nascent style and an introduction to the paradigm shift it portends. Our first object will be to put paid to the symbolic fetishism that monopolised 20th-century discourse about the decorative arts. The current climate crisis calls for a return to material and practical considerations—in other words, for casting off the idealistic superstructures and getting back to the nuts and bolts of the materialist infrastructure. The point is to rediscover the utility value of interior decoration and put together a catalogue of useful decorative devices. After rehearsing the history of these devices and the practical functions they used to perform, we will update the typologies of climate-regulating objects in the light of latter-day scientific findings. The resulting decorative style should be equal to the ecological challenges of the Anthropocene age. For the aim of the Anthropocene style is to reduce the energy consumption of buildings in order to shrink their carbon footprint and their resulting contribution to global warming while concomitantly improving indoor comfort in winter and summer alike. The Anthropocene style features simple passive strategies to cool interiors off during heat waves and, conversely, to capture and retain indoor heat in winter so as to improve domestic comfort without resorting to even more consumption of fossil fuels. This style will, in turn, give rise to new aesthetic values, new forms of beauty.

ACCEPTING HUMAN RESPONSIBILITY FOR GLOBAL WARMING

The oil shocks of the 1970s showed that our modern comfort was wholly dependent on the availability of fossil fuels. Many people had no choice but to turn down the radiators and wear wool sweaters at home, as urged by the French government in 1980.[1] But it wasn't till the 1990s, at the 1992 Rio Earth Summit,[2] that human responsibility for global warming and its disastrous ecological and human consequences came to be officially recognised around the world. It all started back in the industrial age, around 1830, when the first coal-burning factories began emitting greenhouse gases. Ever since, these emissions have been increasingly altering terrestrial and marine ecosystems and even the physical contours of our planet and its atmosphere, the distribution of climates and the shape of coastlines, causing changes in nature

1   See this government ad, for example: *bitly.ws/ByxX*
2   United Nations Framework Convention on Climate Change, UN 1992: *unfccc.int/resource/docs/convkp/conveng.pdf*

that are no longer of local and superficial scope but global and geological. Given the scale of these chemical, physical and biological alterations, affecting the atmosphere and the lithosphere as well, they are regarded by some scientists and thinkers as heralding a change of geological era, from the Holocene to the recently coined 'Anthropocene' epoch.[3] The causes of this sea change are no longer natural, volcanic or cosmic, as in the previous shift from the Pleistocene to the Holocene some 11,700 years ago, but human: specifically, greenhouse gases given off by the combustion of fossil fuels and other industrial activities, as well as deforestation. The resulting upheavals will have far-reaching consequences for human lives and activities, leading to mass migration as coastlines and habitable areas recede, increasingly devastating droughts and floods, changes in local economies and agriculture dependent on specific climatic conditions, and increasingly intense extreme weather events—as well as social unrest and even wars.[4] Since the Rio Summit, curbing greenhouse gas emissions has become a global priority: witness the strenuous concerted efforts to negotiate global accords at subsequent climate conferences like COP 21 (Paris, 2015) and COP 28 (Dubai, 2023).

The buildings and construction sector currently accounts for 39% of CO_2 emissions worldwide[5]—and nearly half here in Europe: 'Heating and cooling in our buildings and industry accounts

3   Crutzen and Stoermer, 2000, pp.17–18
4   Welzer, 2009

for half of the EU's energy consumption', reports the European Commission.[6] To fight global warming in this sector, we must reduce the amount of CO_2 given off by the combustion of fossil fuels, especially in the central heating of buildings, which means reducing the demand for heat.

One-third of CO_2 emissions in the buildings and construction sector (corresponding to 11% of overall CO_2 emissions) are caused by the manufacture and transportation of materials (referred to as the 'carbon footprint' or 'grey energy' of construction materials) and by the actual construction of buildings. The other two-thirds (28% of overall CO_2 emissions) stem from the operation of a building over the course of its lifetime, especially heating, hot water production, air conditioning and lighting—which is why combatting heat loss in poorly insulated buildings is now a big priority. Thermal and energy regulations for the building sector, first introduced in the 1990s, now require twenty centimetres of thermal insulation in the walls of houses to keep the cold out and the heat in.

Other solutions involve reducing the energy consumption of buildings (by improving airtightness and controlling ventilation so the heating can be turned down) and prioritising renewable energy. These are the objectives of various standards and

5   2019 Global Status Report for Buildings and Construction, International Energy Agency (IEA) for the Global Alliance for Buildings and Construction, International Energy Agency (IEA) for the Global Alliance for Buildings and Construction (GlobalABC), 2019: *bitly.ws/xo77*
6   *bitly.ws/Byy3*

labels around the world: Passivhaus[7] in Germany (1996), Minergie[8] in Switzerland (1994), LEED[9] in the US (1993), RT2012[10] (2012) and RE2020[11] (2022) in France, QSAS[12] in Qatar and the different 'green building assessments' in Hong Kong[13] (2009) and Taiwan[14] (1995), to name just a few.

These new thermal standards, regulations and recommendations have far-reaching consequences for architectural design, rendering obsolete many carbon-intensive 20th-century approaches to the outer shape of buildings, construction methods and interior layout.[15] The load-bearing structures of buildings, often made of concrete or steel in the 20th century, have to be thermally insulated with soft wool and relegated to the building's inner recesses. So they no longer form part of a building's visible façade as they did in the 20th century—and before that, in traditional stone, brick and wood architecture—and consequently no longer contribute to a building's aesthetic image at all.

7   The Passivhaus Institut (PHI) was founded in 1996 in Germany by Wolfgang Feist: *passivehouse.com*

8   The Minergie label was founded in 1994 in Switzerland by Ruedi Kriesi and Heinz Uebersax: *minergie.ch*

9   The Leadership in Energy and Environmental Design (LEED) program for green building certification was founded in 1993 by Robert K. Watson, a senior scientist at the Natural Resources Defense Council (NRDC), and is supported by the U.S. Green Building Council (USGBC): *usgbc.org/leed*

10   French Minerstry for Energy Transition: *bitly.ws/xo7u*

11   French Ministry for Energy Transition: *bitly.ws/Byya*

12   Ferwati et al., 2019: *bitly.ws/xo7E*

13   Hong Kong Green Building Council: *bitly.ws/xo7L*

14   Taiwan Architecture & Building Center: *bitly.ws/xo8u*

15   Rahm, 2012

Furthermore, window surfaces have to be down-sized because they overheat in summer (increasing energy consumption for air conditioning) and cool down too fast in winter: even double- and triple-glazed windows let more heat through than a well-insulated opaque wall. What's more, we can't build with concrete anymore the way we did in the 20th century, because of the huge quantities of CO_2 emitted in the production of concrete.[16] This is why we're better off using wood or stone, which, at a glance, immediately signal a change of architectural style, a new era. The 20th century was made of exposed concrete; the 21st century will be made of wood wrapped in thermal insulation.

In the wake of these changes to the building's visible envelope, an element like insulation can be viewed not just as a thermal layer but as a new form of unacknowledged tapestry, inadvertently marking the return of interior decoration. If the minimalist modern style of the 20th century was predicated on fossil fuels and the profligate waste of untold resources and energy, the decarbonisation of building may well usher in a distinctive 21st-century decorative style based on thermal performance, the carbon footprint of materials used and the need to keep interiors cool in summer. These criteria will redefine our formal, material choices and, ultimately, the aesthetic, cultural and social values of Anthropocene-style interiors.

16   Concrete is made of gravel, sand and cement. Cement is made by grinding up various materials, such as clinker, which in turn is produced by sintering different materials, including quicklime (calcium oxide, CaO), in a process called clinkerisation. Quicklime is obtained by heating limestone ($CaCO_3$) to a very high temperature (calcination), which liberates CO_2 as it decomposes into lime (CaO). So the making of concrete actually involves a triple release of CO_2: in the chemical reaction during the calcination of limestone, in the burning of coal to produce the high temperatures (nearly 1500°C) required for calcination, and then in clinkerisation.

HOW MODERNITY
CAST OFF DECORATION

For the present purposes, our interest in the Anthropocene style will be confined to interior design and decoration, or what's known as the 'decorative arts'. For about a century now, this field has been by and large expunged from the architect's job description and left to 'decorators' or, in most cases, the inhabitants themselves. It was Adolf Loos who ushered in this radical reform by proclaiming in 1908 that 'ornament is a crime'.[17] His credo was echoed, albeit somewhat less dogmatically, by Mies van der Rohe's famous dictum 'Less is more.' Le Corbusier then proceeded to reduce interior design to a uniform minimalist coat of 'whitewash'. One's 'home is made clean',[18] he decreed in 1925. 'The hierarchical tradition of decoration has collapsed. [...] Gilding is fading out. [...] Modern decorative art is not decorated. [...] Decorative art has no reason to exist.'[19]

17   Loos, [1908] 2015
18   Le Corbusier, 1925
19   *Ibid.*

Thus, modernity disqualified the decorative arts and banished curtains and drapery, panelling and marquetry, padding and upholstery, rugs, wallpaper, folding screens, baseboards, mouldings, chandeliers and mirrors, writing them off as a superfluous excess of interior decoration that served no purpose whatsoever. This surfeit of ornament was to give way to minimal, neutral and often white interior design, reduced to the plainest possible expression of the architectural construction thanks to the novel capabilities of modern technical equipment, of mechanical and electrical systems of heating, ventilation and artificial lighting that emerged in the late 19th century. Over the course of the 20th century, the very word *decoration* took on a censorious, even derisive, connotation of superficial frivolity.[20] This purge of the 19th-century art of interior design—again, made possible by massive use of fossil fuels—laid the foundation for the modernist aesthetic, the 'modern style' that reigned supreme throughout the 20th century and whose asceticism has long been equated with good taste among architects.[21] Seeing as decoration serves no practical purpose, it has long been customary in our profession to condemn or deride decoration and its futility in the spirit of Adolf Loos, and to consign such superficial concerns to decorators, interior designers and amateurs, as well as to home decor magazines for the general public and 'trend books', all of which flourish by purveying curtains

20   Soulillou, 1992, pp.117–138
21   See, e.g., *bitly.ws/xo8N*

and wall hangings in elegant hues and fine fabrics, mirrors and lamps, as an aesthetic realm unto itself, self-referential, most of the time narrative and metaphorical, often traditionalist and superficial,[22] devoid of any practical purpose, serving merely to 'decorate' homes, not to warm them up or cool them down anymore. It may be observed in passing that this cultural phenomenon was highly gendered, with interior decoration writ large on the pages of women's magazines, for example, in the 20th century.

The modernists were behind this shift from the practical to the symbolic. At the heart of his 1929 Barcelona Pavilion, for instance, Mies van der Rohe chose red onyx to evoke the warmth of the departed fireplace and used a rug to symbolise the perimeter of the static space of the erstwhile living room, which was now dissolved into the spatial continuum of the pavilion. Rugs would henceforth be stripped of any practical function and laid on floors already warmed by the coils of central heating beneath them, to serve merely symbolic purposes. And the heavy curtains on the windows to block the draughts and keep the cold out would be reduced to sheer curtains serving merely to preserve a certain domestic intimacy, their thermal function supplanted by a social function.

But who actually created this specific modernist style? Who first invented this rarefied minimalist decorative art that was to become a hallmark of the 20th century? Was it Adolf Loos,

---

22   *bitly.ws/xo8V*

Le Corbusier, Eileen Gray, Mies van der Rohe, Walter Gropius? Our preferred answer to this idealistic anthropocentric question of history is a dialectical materialism that views stylistic and aesthetic revolutions in relation to changes in physical conditions of a 'geological, hydrographical, climatic' or other nature.[23] After all, isn't coal the actual author of all this, the real designer of the modernity that made it possible to replace human effort with the production of heat energy?[24] Wasn't it thanks to fossil fuels, which made central heating and air conditioning possible, that decorative art could be brushed aside after the turn of the century and struck off the serious architect's mandate? Isn't electricity to blame for stripping chandeliers and gilding of their practical utility? And wasn't it central heating that spelled the demise of tapestries to ward off the cold, leaving nothing but their ornamental and social functions of embellishing

23   Karl Marx, Friedrich Engels and Joseph Weydemeyer, *The German Ideology*, 1845: 'The first premise of all human history is, of course, the existence of living human individuals. Thus the first fact to be established is the physical organization of these individuals and their consequent relation to the rest of nature. Of course, we cannot here go either into the actual physical nature of man, or into the natural conditions in which man finds himself—geological, hydrographical, climatic and so on. The writing of history must always set out from these natural bases and their modification in the course of history through the action of men.'
24   See Robert A. Millikan, *Human Origins*, vol. 11, New York, 1933, pp.134–135: 'If, then, you ask me to put into one sentence the cause of that recent rapid and enormous change I should reply: "It is found in the discovery and utilization of the means by which heat energy can be made to do man's work for him."'

the home and impressing one's guests? Weren't Adolf Loos, Le Corbusier, Mies van der Rohe and Walter Gropius really just spokespeople for fossil fuels, and wasn't modernist style just the aesthetic expression of coal?

And what about our day and age? Who is behind the aesthetic revolution we are now witnessing and participating in, which is enveloping buildings in thermal insulation and trading concrete, aluminium and fibreglass in for stone, wood and straw? Am I the one driving the decarbonisation of architecture, in both the construction (grey energy) of buildings and their operation (energy efficiency), by means of this tract? Or is it rather the greenhouse gases that cause global warming? Once again, if coal paved the way for the modernist style of the early 20th century, it is CO_2 that is now paving the way for the Anthropocene style of the early 21st century.

WHY DECORATIVE ART WAS NOT DECORATIVE BEFORE THE ADVENT OF FOSSIL FUELS

The divorce between architecture and interior design, between utility and embellishment, objectivity and subjectivity, went by and large unchallenged after the birth of modernism.[25] But nowadays we're seeing an unlooked-for reconciliation of these oppositions in the application of the new (Minergie-, RE2020- or Passivhaus-type) energy efficiency standards. For if the minimalist white neutrality of the modernist style prevailed for such a long time after the 1932 MoMA exhibition of modern architecture,[26] it was owing to the late 19th-century invention of central heating, whose radiators subsequently stripped decorative interior design of its *raison d'être*. The Farnsworth

25   This divorce can be traced back to 1933, when the Nazis shuttered the Bauhaus (where the textile arts of curtain, tapestry and rug making were fused under the direction of Anni Albers, followed by Gunta Stölzl and Lily Reich, and the art of building construction under the direction of Walter Gropius, followed by Hannes Meyer and Mies van der Rohe).
26   *Modern Architecture: International Exhibition, New York, February 10 to March 23, 1932,* Museum of Modern Art, New York

House by Ludwig Mies van der Rohe, completed in 1951, is a case in point: Its oil-fired boiler, hidden out of sight in the house's only opaque room, heats the house through a grid of invisible hot-water coils under the floor. As a result, the façade could be fully glazed, which would have been impossible with heating by means of non-fossil fuels, such as a wood-burning fireplace, because glass lets too much cold through and the house would have been freezing cold in wintertime.[27]

What was the decorative art of the past if not a strategy set to improve the lighting and thermal comfort of the cold, dark interiors of old buildings? Pre-20th-century Northern Europeans, for example, laid wool rugs on the floor to stave off the cold coming up through conduction. These low-emissivity wool rugs constituted a rudimentary version of the kind of thermal insulation we use today.[28] Likewise, tapestries and other wall coverings as well as woodwork were used to fend off the cold radiating from walls of old stone or brick, materials with high thermal conductivity.[29] Curtains were used to cover poorly sealed joints

27   See the heating and ventilating sections and plans for the Farnsworth House in the MoMA collection: *bitly.ws/Byyn*
28   See Rahm, 2020, chap. 5
29   See Eugène Müntz, *La tapisserie,* Paris, A. Quantin, 1890, p.14: *'Sans aller aussi loin que Semper, on admettra sans difficulté que la destination première des tissus appliqués à l'architecture (tentures disposées verticalement, tapis étendus sur le sol) a été de protéger tour à tour contre le soleil et contre le froid.'* ['Without going as far as Semper, we may readily concede that the initial purpose of fabrics applied to architecture (vertical hangings, rugs laid on the floor) was to protect against the sun and against the cold by turns.']

between the walls and the frames of old windows or doors that let draughts through. Nowadays, (Tyvek-type[30]) air seals made of synthetic plastic, the kind used in Minergie-certified buildings,[31] have proved extremely effective at preventing leakage of warm air in winter and cold air in summer, thereby minimising heating and air-conditioning requirements. Back in the day, to make up for the very high conductivity of the old single-glazed windows, heavy velvet drapes were drawn closed at night to keep the indoor heat from being sucked out the window by radiation and up into the heavenly vault. The indoor air was warmed by radiation, convection and conduction, through the use of fireplaces, stoves, foot warmers and warming pans, all of which were functional elements of interior decoration—even domestic animals were kept indoors to add warmth.[32] Likewise, mirrors, gilded objects and fittings, chandeliers and myriad forms of glittering glasswork once served to enhance the faint sunlight seeping in through the small windows and the dim light of flickering candle flames by reflecting, diffracting and refracting the light and increasing the illuminated surface area and the intensity of the light.[33] In a word, all decorative art had a practical function, which the current climate crisis now impels us to rediscover.

30   DuPont de Nemours: *bitly.ws/xo9r*

31   Airtightness guideline for Minergie buildings (RiLuMi): *bitly.ws/xo9C*

32   See Benoît Garnot, *La culture matérielle en France aux XVIe , XVIIe et XVIIIe siècles*, Paris, Ophrys, 2000, p.77: *'Pour renforcer leurs défenses contre le froid, les citadins utilisent divers accessoires remplis de braise (braseros, chaufferettes pour les pieds, bassinoires et bouillottes pour les lits…), et surtout ils cherchent à limiter les courants d'air avec des tentures murales et des rideaux, des portières et des paravents.'* ['To reinforce their defences against the cold, city dwellers made use of various accessories filled with embers (braziers, foot warmers, warming pans and hot-water bottles for their beds…), and above all they sought to curtail draughts by means of wall hangings and curtains, portieres and folding screens.']

33   See Nadine Ribet, *Feu—ami ou ennemi?*, Paris, Dunod, 2018, p.69: *'La recherche de plus de luminosité explique l'usage de la dorure et, à partir du XVIIIe siècle, le goût pour les boiseries et les plafonds peints en blanc et la multiplication des miroirs.'* ['The desire for more light accounts for the use of gilding and, from the 18th century on, the predilection for woodwork and ceilings painted white and for multiple mirrors.']

HOW FOSSIL FUELS STRIPPED
INTERIORS DOWN

The decorative art of ages past was rendered obsolete and superfluous by easy access to energy from coal, oil and natural gas in the 19th century, followed by the electrification of homes in the 20th century (from around 1920), the late 19th-century invention of central heating systems and radiators, which use hot water in pipes as a thermal conductor to heat indoor air (the first such system in France was installed in 1877 at the castle in Le Pecq, near Paris[34]), and the invention of electrical air conditioning by Willis Carrier in 1902 and its popularisation from the 1950s on.

We realise today that energy consumption was no object in the design of these stripped-down, 'modern-style' 20th-century interiors, which were often poorly insulated (if at all before 1970) and had outsized windows (single glazed before Thomas Stetson's invention of thermally insulating double glazing in 1965). Considerations of energy were

34   BNF Passerelles: *bitly.ws/xo9Z*

wholly confined to its use in central heating, electric lighting and air conditioning during an age of affordable oil prices.[35] Hence the contention by architecture critics like Siegfried Giedion in 1948[36] and Reyner Banham in 1969[37] that building technologies (heating, ventilation, plumbing, electricity) had become more essential to the definition of architecture and its various forms in the 20th century than its load-bearing structures (walls and floors), let alone interior decoration (rugs, curtains and tapestries). The most iconic illustration there of is the Centre Pompidou, by the architects Renzo Piano and Richard Rogers, which was completed in 1977, with its pipes and ventilation ducts incorporated into its 'inside-out' façade. This building's aesthetic image turns away from its construction, its load-bearing structure and statics, to flamboyantly display its mechanised systems of electricity, water and air flows instead, through colour-coded pipes, ducts and conduits. But these modern heating and air-conditioning technologies are dependent on a constant and unlimited energy supply and have given rise to extensively glazed buildings without thermal inertia or insulation, which are no longer adapted to our day and age. They consume too much energy, 85% of which still comes from fossil fuels like natural gas and fuel oil.

35   Oil was very easily accessible, and therefore cheap, until the 1970s. But new, more complicated and more expensive drilling methods (oil rigs, fracking) were subsequently required to get at crude oil.
36   Giedion, 1948
37   Banham, 1969

When burned to heat water for radiators or to cool the air, these fuels give off CO_2, which is opaque to infrared radiation in the atmosphere, thereby engendering the greenhouse effect that's behind global warming. Like so many other poorly insulated pre-1990s buildings, the Centre Pompidou has been described as a 'heat sieve'. And it's going to be shuttered from late 2023 to sometime in 2027 for a top-to-bottom overhaul, including thermal insulation,[38] to reduce its energy consumption.

38   See Jean-Christophe Castelain, 'Le Centre Pompidou fermera pendant 3 ans en 2023', *Le journal des arts,* 26 January 2021: *bitly.ws/xoab*

INTERIOR DECORATION ONCE
KEPT OUT THE COLD

Traditional interior decoration before the advent of central heating served a climate agenda. To keep their feet warm, people laid rugs under their chairs, by their bedsides, wherever their feet would otherwise be in contact with a chilly stone, terracotta or clay floor, so as to prevent heat loss by thermal conductivity. Since cold comes up from the floor, our early ancestors used to lay straw on the floor, on which to sleep fully clothed. The first wool rugs to appear in Western interiors were a gift to Charlemagne (albeit less well known than the legendary white elephant sent to Aachen) from the Abbasid caliph of Baghdad Harun al-Rashid in 798 CE.[39] The thermal performance of wool fibres, which trap tiny air pockets to highly insulating effect, is exactly the same as that of our rockwool, fibreglass or hemp insulation, which resists the transfer of heat between inside and outside the building. Another advantage of wool rugs has to do

39   De Viel-Castel, 1864

with 'thermal effusivity'—i.e., a material's ability to exchange heat through direct contact with another material. The higher a material's effusivity, the faster and more efficient the exchange of heat: a good example is marble in old Italian churches, whose coldness is readily transferred to churchgoers in summer cooling their bodies upon contact. The lower the thermal effusivity of a material (e.g., wood or, even lower, wool), the slower and more limited the exchange of heat with its surroundings.

Tapestries function likewise. The stone walls of medieval castles were covered with tapestries, initially also of Middle Eastern provenance.[40] Before the development of modern heating technologies, tapestries—along with other kinds of wall coverings, hangings and panelling—formed a thermal barrier against cold masonry walls of brick, stone or concrete blocks, all of which are extremely thermally conductive and easily penetrated by the outside cold. Like wool rugs and wood floors, tapestries provide a layer of insulation. They also change the emissivity coefficient of the surface to which the human body is exposed. A material's emissivity,[41] a physical value between 0 and 1,[42] is a measure of its ability to absorb and emit infrared radiation at the same time. The more a given material's temperature radiates and is communicated to objects around it, the higher its emissivity

40   Alexandre, 1892
41   *sciencedirect.com/topics/engineering/emissivity*
42   For a table of emissivity values, see *bitly.ws/xoar*

(the closer it gets to the maximum value of 1); the more a material tends to retain its heat, the lower its emissivity (approaching 0).[43] A cold wall 'diffuses' its cold in the winter if made of highly emissive material. Conversely, a low-emissivity wall will remain neutral, so bodies in the vicinity won't lose their heat to the wall. Human skin is extremely emissive (0.99), which means it heats up very fast under infrared radiation and, conversely, loses a great deal of heat when exposed to a cold emissive surface.

The 19th-century German architect Gottfried Semper[44] postulated that the essential 'elements' of architecture are the hearth (i.e., fire), roof (ceiling or canopy), 'mound' (floor, box spring or mattress) and enclosure (curtains, partition, tapestry or bed hangings). These 'four elements of architecture' also happen to be four elements of interior decoration. Curtains are an extremely common decorative element, whose practical function has been largely forgotten. Prior to the 20th century, the joints between the masonry wall and the wooden window frame were imperfect and would let in cold air, sometimes even rain and snow. The unpleasant resulting draughts came to be called *vent-coulis* (i.e., 'flowing wind') in French because they have a cooling effect by convection,[45] which is another mode of heat exchange between an

43 *Handbook of Chemistry and Physics,* Cleveland, Chemical Rubber Publishing Co., 1972
44 Semper, [1834-1869] 2007
45 Pierre Richelet, *Dictionnaire de la langue françoise, ancienne et moderne,* Paris, 1728

object and a fluid environment such as air or water. A draught cools the skin down by accelerating the loss of body heat: our 37°C is gone with the wind—or rather, with a strong draught. Even when curtains are open, they can cover the joint between the window frame and the wall through which a cold draught seeps in. They are windscreens, so to speak, slowing the influx of air.[46] Curtains were designed to be floor length so the trim at the bottom would 'stop draughts more than stop light'.[47] The curtains, wall coverings and doors of yore, whilst creating an atmosphere of cosy intimacy, were above all 'primitive' air-sealing devices that prefigured the airtightness required nowadays to meet the latest thermal standards (e.g., once again, Minergie[48] and Passivhaus[49]): then as now, the point was to keep cold outdoor air from entering heated interiors in winter.

46 *Ibid: 'Paravent: C'est un ouvrage de Menuisier et de Tapissier pour mettre dans une chambre l'hiver, afin d'empêcher le vent qui vient de la porte.'* ['Folding screen: A work of Carpentry and Tapestry to be placed in a room during the winter, to block the wind coming from the door.']
47 Duvette, Volle, Walter, 2016
48 Airtightness guideline for Minergie buildings (RiLuMi): *bitly.ws/xo9C*
49 'L'étanchéité à l'air de nos bâtiments': *bitly.ws/xoaz*

CRYSTAL CHANDELIERS ONCE
SERVED A PURPOSE

A number of decorative devices were initially designed to make up for the dim artificial lighting at night and the meagre sunlight admitted by small windows by day. From the Middle Ages to the 19th century, various devices served to increase, enhance and diffract the faint light supplied by candles or, more frequently because less expensive, the fire in the hearth.[50] 'Besides their aesthetic aspect, gilded decorations reflected candlelight well', wrote Louis Figuier, a 19th-century French populariser of science. 'In the second half of the 17th century, mirrors were also introduced to interiors, serving especially to increase the brightness of the lights.'[51] The dozens of bevelled crystal pendants in a single chandelier serve as so many tiny mirrors reflecting the light and magically redoubling the number of candles and the light's intensity.

50   For a history of indoor lighting, see Louis Figuier, *L'art de l'éclairage*, Paris, Jouvet et Cie, 1887
51   *Ibid.*

But this whole decorative language of gilding, mirrors, crystals and ornamental glassware was to be eclipsed by the more effective 20th-century artifice of electric lighting. These crystals and gold decorations were stripped of any functional raison d'être by incandescent bulbs and fluorescent tubes. Written off by modernism (1900-1960), they were then relegated—once their original function had been forgotten—to the nebulous subjective domain of personal preferences characteristic of late postmodernism (1980-2019).

MODERNITY AND THE DEMISE OF FUNCTIONAL DECORATION

In short, all the elements of interior decoration that had previously—from prehistory to the very end of the 19th century—served to improve living conditions in dwellings that could be likened to 'thermal sieves' were subsequently reduced to matters of subjective personal taste. Decoration disappeared from modern interiors in the 20th century or took a purely metaphorical or poetic turn, as in 1980s designs by the Memphis Group or Garouste and Bonetti, for example, largely owing to the invention of central heating and the hot-water radiator in 1877. Beginning in the latter half of the 19th century, the use of coal as a fuel had profoundly altered Western societies and led to a revolution in the forms, materials and dimensions of architecture.[52] Instead of wood being burned in fireplaces, which had never been very effective at heating human habitations,[53] coal was now mined and burned in

52   Rahm, 2020, chap. 4
53   Jandot, 2017

boilers that were installed in the cellar. The boiler could heat water to over 60°C and send it up to the radiators, which, through conduction and, to a lesser extent, radiation, raised indoor air temperatures more than ever before in human history—and far more easily, efficiently and satisfactorily at that. Since the invention of the steam engine by James Watt in 1770, the combustion of fossil fuels has increased the amount of available energy by a factor of 200.[54] Widespread access to this power from the combustion of coal, then from gas, oil and nuclear fission in the 20th century, rendered the climate-regulating devices of the industrial era wholly superfluous. What was the use of hanging tapestries in the home now that rooms were heated by radiators carrying piping hot water that was continuously produced by a coal- or oil-fired boiler? Once they'd lost their use value, the old decorative elements served no function save that of ornamentation.

54   Morris, 2017

THE RETURN OF FUNCTIONAL DECORATION TO COPE WITH GLOBAL WARMING

Since the first oil crisis in 1973, thermal strategies to reduce energy consumption in buildings have been steadily advancing, giving rise to a number of laws[55] and standards that chiefly concern the building envelope (i.e., the façade) and its general heating and ventilation systems. In consequence, research has hitherto focused on 'outside' architecture, on improving the thermal insulation and airtightness of façades, controlling the indoor air renewal system for the whole building, and not on the interior design, furniture and decoration of individual homes. Modifying individual interiors, which is clearly a simpler and quicker expedient, can provide an alternative or complementary approach to reducing a whole building's CO_2 emissions but is sometimes hindered by the sheer complexity of the applicable standards and the sheer bulkiness of

---

55 E.g., the Swiss canton of Vaud's environmental law on energy: *bitly.ws/Byyx*

the exterior architecture. We feel that the time has come for interior design to be reinstated in its former functional role to help to limit global warming.

So to this end we have drawn up a brief inventory of climate-regulating and energy-saving interior decoration, a catalogue of decorative solutions for the 21st century. In France, for example, the first thermal regulations (called RT1974) were introduced in response to the 1973 oil crisis. The goal was to reduce the energy consumption of buildings to below 225 kWh/m²/yr. Buildings erected between 1950 and 1970 consumed an estimated 300 kWh/m²/yr. Here in Switzerland, the SIA 180 standard[56] regulates the thermal insulation of buildings nationwide.[57] The target 'U value'[58] of thermal transmittance (i.e., the rate of heat transfer through a structure) set in 1988 was significantly lowered in 1999 in the 180/1 version[59] and then again in 2014.[60] This standard aims to limit new buildings' energy consumption to at most one-eighth of that in pre-1974 'thermal sieves', back in the days when you had to burn eight times as much oil or gas as in 2014 to heat the same floor space. To bring energy consumption all the way down to

56 *bitly.ws/xoaJ*
57 This standard chiefly concerns the thickness of the insulation: the thicker it is, the lower the U value and the better the insulation.
58 'The U value (also known as "U factor" or "U coefficient") indicates the ability of building elements (walls, floors, roofs, windows, etc.) and insulating materials to resist this heat transfer. It is measured in units of W/(m²K). The lower a material's U value, the better it insulates.' *bitly.ws/Byyz*
59 *bitly.ws/xoaR*
60 *bitly.ws/xoaU*

this low target, a building's walls, windows, floor slabs and roof have to be well insulated so as to prevent the heat emitted by the radiators from escaping. All materials have a thermal conductivity value, commonly denoted by λ (lambda) or k, which is measured in watts per metre-kelvin (W(mK)). The higher this value is, the more heat the material in question conducts. The lower it is, the better the material insulates (by inhibiting the transfer of heat from one side of its width to the other). Metals conduct heat well—which is why radiators are made of cast iron (50 W(mK)) or steel (46 W(mK)), so as to rapidly transmit the (50°C) heat of the water flowing through them to the surrounding rooms. To keep cold air out of our homes, the loadbearing materials (which are often highly heat conductive) need to be lined with an insulating material—i.e., a material that contains a lot of air (λ value of 0.0262 W(mK)) and has an extremely low density. What matters is not the nature of the material but its porosity, the relative volume of microscopic air bubbles trapped between its fibres. The thermal conductivity of rockwool or glass wool (i.e., fibreglass), for example, is 0.035 W(mK). To determine the thickness of the thermal insulation layer to be applied to an element of a building's supporting structure, one must also calculate the material's thermal transmittance (U value in W/[m²K]) based on its thermal conductivity (λ value in W(mK)) for a given thickness. The 2014 version of the SIA 180 standard sets the upper limit of U values for the opaque parts of new buildings at 0.17 W/(m²K),[61] which corresponds to a layer of thermal insulation 23 centimetres thick. More stringent standards, like those of Minergie and Passivhaus, require even lower thermal conductivity values for walls, roofs, windows and floor slabs, to achieve a U value of 0.15 W/(m²K) for opaque elements, for example, which means enveloping the load-bearing structure of a standard construction with a thermal insulation layer 26 centimetres thick.[62]

61   *bitly.ws/xoaU*
62   Precise calculations are made by HVAC and sanitation design offices, but we can roughly estimate how thick thermal insulation needs to be using a calculator of this sort: *ubakus.de/en/r-value-calculator/*

THERMAL INSULATION AS NOVEL 21ST-CENTURY DECORATIVE ELEMENT

These thermal requirements are revolutionising the art of building in the 21st century. Insulating buildings has turned out to be a priority for reducing the conductivity of façades, roofs and windows and using less energy to heat more. In France, for instance, buildings constructed to RT2012 standards (effective to the end of 2021) consume 50 kWh/m²/yr, which is one-sixth of the figure (300 kWh/m²/yr) for uninsulated buildings back in 1970. The new RE2020 thermal standard, an environmental regulation in effect since January 2022, aims to cut energy consumption even further, to 12 kWh/m²/yr, which is 1/25th of the 1970 levels. And energy consumption is as low as 1/300th of 1970 levels for so-called positive-energy buildings (BEPOS), which produce more energy than they consume, if they are perfectly insulated and generate power (electricity and hot water) by means of solar or photovoltaic panels.

A perfectly thermally insulated building would mean no heat loss at all. And what is thermal insulation if not a remarkable comeback of tapestries and rugs? The austere modern minimalism of 20th-century architecture, with its thin walls and large windows, is clearly out of step with 21st-century thermal requirements. Concerted efforts to decarbonise our built environment are now instead bringing us back to the fundamentals of architecture in order to keep out the cold, the dark, the wind and the damp.

HOW TO REDUCE ENERGY CONSUMPTION AND CO_2 EMISSIONS

In the aftermath of the 1992 Earth Summit in Rio de Janeiro, research in building physics and energy that had been launched in the wake of the 1970s oil crises resumed at Swiss universities of applied sciences—e.g., at LESBAT (Laboratory of Solar Energetics and Building Physics)[63] and in the 2000-Watt Society program at ETH Zurich.[64] The object of this research was essentially to reduce energy consumption in the operation of buildings and to improve the building envelope's thermal efficiency. The findings were applied two years later with the launch of the Minergie label in Switzerland.[65] This initial research on the operational performance of buildings (HVAC: heating, ventilation and air conditioning) and the thermal performance of building envelopes has been successfully applied and gradually supplemented by research on the grey

63   *lesbat.ch*
64   *bitly.ws/xobt*
65   *bitly.ws/ByyI*

energy of buildings—i.e., the 'embodied energy' (also known as 'embodied carbon') in materials that is required to manufacture and transport and eventually to deconstruct and dispose of them. As the problems of a building's operational (HVAC) emissions and of its envelope's thermal efficiency (which account for two-thirds of a building's energy consumption) have been addressed and alleviated, grey energy (accounting for one-third of a building's energy consumption) has become proportionally more significant and now accounts for half of the problem.[66]

So much for efforts to improve buildings as a whole—that is to say, their 'exterior' design. But what about their interior design? What kinds of materials and formal approaches will reduce CO_2 emissions while improving thermal comfort inside the home? Can we use interior design to improve a building's energy efficiency by insulating on the inside when outside insulation is not an option, e.g. when we're not allowed to alter the façade of a building "listed" as a historical monument?

66   Röck et al., 2020

FORMS AND MATERIALS
OF THE ANTHROPOCENE STYLE

Given its tremendous carbon footprint, the buildings and construction sector is key to the fight against global warming. The current change of geological epoch is a paradigm shift that calls for the decarbonisation of architectural aesthetics, a new chapter in the history of decorative arts and architectural styles. After the Regency, Louis XV, Empire and Louis Philippe styles, after the modern and postmodern styles, the purpose of the Anthropocene style is to provide thermal comfort indoors in winter as in summer without requiring any electricity—in other words, passively—making use solely of the physical features of materials, of sound, low-carbon devices that help reduce a building's energy consumption and, consequently, its CO_2 emissions. This style is to be elegant and beautiful (its aesthetic values will catch on under its own steam, so to speak), like any decorative style that came before. It is to be innovative and contemporary, updating the art of interior design and decoration to meet the current challenges of sustainable development and to reduce energy consumption and greenhouse gas emissions. Interior designers will now have to rethink decoration and redesign the lines, patterns and geometries of decorative elements to be applied to walls, ceilings, floors and windows, to come up with a new decorative art to improve thermal comfort. We will have to reinvent the traditional flooring layout, woodwork and rugs, the shapes and materials of mouldings and baseboards according to the optical behaviour of sunbeams in order to enhance the natural sunlight and avoid the use of electric lighting, to absorb and phase-shift infrared heat so as to avoid over-heating during the day and retrieve by conduction the excess heat that has accumulated under the ceiling in order to warm up the room at night in winter. We will seek to lower the thermal conductivity coefficient of walls and avoid thermal bridges so as to keep cold air out in winter and keep warm air in and, the other way around in summer, keep the heat out and the cool air in. We will select materials according to their physical, optical and thermal properties, their carbon footprint, their water vapor permeability and air porosity, their thermal conductivity, diffusivity, emissivity and effusivity. We'll make a point of choosing materials and

67   Albedo is a theoretical value between 0 and 1 representing a material's ability to reflect heat from solar radiation. At 0, all the solar radiation is converted into heat upon contact with the material, which rises in temperature as a result. This material will necessarily be black, for the colour black means that it does not reflect any wavelength of incident light. At 1, the material reflects all the sun's rays and their energy, so it remains cold.

colours according to their albedo,[67] their textures and their effects on thermal comfort. The colour palette of the materials will be chosen carefully so as to reflect infrared in some places and absorb it or let it pass through in others, while simultaneously reflecting the short wavelengths of visible white light or absorbing them in order to benefit from their heat as well.

What should be put on the floor when it's cold outside? Wool, given its low thermal effusivity. And when it's hot outside? Copper or marble, given their high thermal effusivity. Can we recover the heat from sun rays hitting the floor in the wintertime and the heat that accumulates under the ceiling? What should be put on the walls if they're cold? What kind of floor covering will cool down the interior in the summertime? Can nighttime coolness be stored in the summer using a folding screen with high thermal inertia so it will radiate that coolness during a heat wave?

Fossil fuels having made it possible to build and decorate the same way anywhere on the globe, decorative aesthetics will henceforth vary in line with the climate and the season. Across-the-board approaches will give way to specific, geographically localised decorative solutions to keep homes cooler in summer and in the tropics and warmer in winter and closer to the poles. We will explore passive decorative solutions (tapestries, rugs, folding screens, etc.) to warm up our homes in winter even while reducing the use of radiators. And we will look for passive solutions to cool off our homes in summer (despite the expected increased frequency of heat waves)—e.g., infrared-reflecting wall coverings, high-effusivity flooring (marble, metal), low-emissivity curtains—with a view to forgoing, or at least markedly reducing, the use of air conditioning in the future.

For our present purposes, the Anthropocene style concerns the decorative part of architecture—in other words, the temporary seasonal coverings applied to the load-bearing structures of a building: these elements traditionally comprise tapestries and wall coverings, rugs, mirrors, folding screens, curtains, etc. This style will also apply to more permanent interior decoration: gilded fittings and fixtures, woodwork, facings, mouldings, cornices, reliefs, panelling and wainscoting, wallpaper, padding, etc. The Anthropocene style is a formalised decorative art for warding off the cold and darkness in Western interiors. It also involves updating various other decorative strategies introduced in the late 19th century to fend off infectious diseases: viz., coating walls with washable enamel paint or disinfectant whitewash, using door handles and handrails made of virucidal copper and placing a basin at the entrance for washing hands, among other things.

SOME EXAMPLES OF
THE ANTHROPOCENE STYLE

What should we put on our floors, walls and ceilings? What materials and forms will warm up our homes in winter without our having to turn on the radiator and cool off our homes in summer without our having to turn on the AC? What can be added to enhance indoor light in winter without consuming more electricity? How can indoor air be detoxified? What colour should the walls be painted to keep them—and us—cool? Each item of Anthropocene art is a new surface decoration whose physical performance will improve the thermal and sanitary properties, air quality and lighting of indoor areas even while reducing energy consumption. Consequently, we will define the forms and materiality of new decorative elements according to what they produce in the way of heat and air flows, conduction and convection, and their optical behaviour with regard to visible light and infrared waves, depending on the material and its thickness, on certain surfaces, in or on certain other materials—always with a view to improving comfort and cutting down on energy consumption.

A material's effusivity, emissivity and thermal conductivity values are key tools for curbing energy consumption in the fight against global warming. We will choose an extremely insulative material for our building's façade, for example, and a material with low emissivity for the walls in order to keep from losing body heat by radiation to the colder walls around us in wintertime. We'll opt for wool on the floor in winter to avoid losing heat by thermal conduction. In summer, on the other hand, marble floors, as recommended by architects back in the Renaissance, won't draw away our excess heat by conduction, thanks to their high thermal effusivity.

To decorate interiors, we'll choose the alloys and other materials best suited to achieving our energy-saving goals. We'll develop architectural and interior design solutions using these new materials in nonstructural, removable or permanent decorative elements, for which we may have to come up with new names, uses and methods of installation or application. We'll identify the physical properties that determine a material's thermal and optical values—viz., its conductivity, emissivity, effusivity, diffusivity and albedo—in relation to its density and specific heat capacity. These characteristics will enable us to redefine design choices according to climate and energy-saving objectives.

To reduce CO_2 emissions in winter, we need to lower our energy consumption by turning the heating down or off. Here are a few new types of decorative elements we're likely to find in the energy-efficient homes of the future:

1 **Low-thermal-effusivity rugs**
   To ward off the cold in the wintertime, we recommend rugs made of materials with the lowest possible thermal effusivity, which won't remove body heat by thermal conduction. These rugs can be rolled out in winter to keep warm and then rolled back up and stowed away in summer to cool off.

2 **Low-emissivity curtains**
   These curtains are to be hung just a few centimetres from the cold exterior walls. They will be made of a material with extremely low emissivity that 'reflects' the coldness radiat-

ing from the exterior walls back onto those walls, thereby preventing our body heat from radiating towards the cold walls.

3 **Low-emissivity mirrors**
The object is to design mirrors that reflect infrared but not visible light, thereby reflecting the infrared heat radiated by human bodies back onto them to warm us up in winter.

4 **Low-thermal-conductivity tapestries**
We recommend hanging tapestries about twenty centimetres thick on cold walls. They should be made of the most thermally insulating materials available so as not to conduct the coldness of the exterior walls into the indoor air.

5 **Airtight folding screens**
Screens made of the most airtight material available are to be placed in front of the front door, windows and vents to block draughts that cool the skin by convection—i.e., by preventing the heat generated by the human body from remaining on the surface of the skin and warming it.

6 **Spectral-light lamps**
We recommend lamps whose spectrum is confined to the wavelengths visible to the human eye—i.e., the colours to which the three types of cones, or photoreceptor cells, on the human retina are most sensitive, peaking at

560 nm, 530 nm and 420 nm. These lamps will help cut down on energy consumption.

7   Convective chairs

Warm air rises because it's lighter than cold air, whereas cold air sinks towards the floor. When the indoor temperature drops, a convective chair will raise the body towards the heat gathering under the ceiling.

Thus, the materials for these decorative art objects in the Anthropocene style will be selected expressly for physical behaviours that are ideally suited to their functions with regard to the flow of air, heat and light. Their forms will depend on where they are to be placed in a given room according to the natural supply of radiant heat from the sun and daily variations in the temperature of the walls. Furthermore, the materials must have a small carbon footprint. For example, low-effusivity tapestries will be made of cellulose wadding (grey energy: 1.95 kWh/kg) rather than glass wool (grey energy: 13.83 kWh/kg).[68]

68   Calculations by Bruno Jarno / Association Arcanne

'Over 40°C in the cities, long periods of drought and very little snow in winter: in forty years' time, Switzerland might come to resemble a Mediterranean country today', a Swiss journalist predicted in 2018.[69] 'If greenhouse gas emissions continue to rise unchecked', the Swiss National Centre for Climate Services warned that same year, 'a further increase in the annual average temperature of around 2–3°C is possible by the middle of this century.'[70] These are plausible scenarios,[71] which would mean an increase in summer temperatures of up to 4.4°C by 2050—and as much as 7.2°C by 2100.[72] The toll that would take

69   Luigi Jorio, 'Torrid Time Predicted for Switzerland by 2060', Swissinfo, 2018: *bitly.ws/ByyX*
70   Swiss National Centre for Climate Services (NCCS), CH2018 Climate Change Scenarios: *bitly.ws/Byz5*
71   Hansjakob Baumgartner, 'Chaleur estivale: Comment rafraîchir les villes', Swiss Federal Office for the Environment, 29 May 2019: *bitly.ws/xobT*
72   NCCS: *bitly.ws/xobM*

on human health is obvious: 'Excessive heat poses health risks, especially for the very old and the very young. Very hot summers have increased mortality rates, essentially due to cardiovascular diseases.'[73]

Faced with this reality, interior design based on scientific and technical principles of energy and building physics can help by recommending rugs, tapestries and curtains which, unlike those used to warm interiors in winter, can actually lower the risks of overheating in summertime. Interior design in the Anthropocene can draw on the traditional practice of passive solutions that don't require any mechanical or electrical devices. The point is to give people who are liable to suffer from the heat a set of simple, practical, temporary solutions involving passive decoration to use without resorting to air conditioning, which exacerbates global warming.

Let's imagine four items that could limit the rise in indoor temperatures during a heat wave:

8   Low-thermal-emissivity curtains
We propose coating curtains on the outside with a material of very low thermal emissivity (e.g., polished aluminium [e=0.05], tin [e=0.05] or polished brass [e=0.03]). When the sun is shining in through the window in summer, these coated curtains will reflect the

73 '975 heat-related deaths were reported during the 2003 heat wave in Switzerland. In the summer of 2015, the second-hottest summer since measurements began in 1864, nearly 800 people died for the same reasons.' Baumgartner: *bitly.ws/xobT*

visible and infrared solar radiation back towards the exterior, thereby preventing the influx of solar heat.

9 Thermal-inertia screens or tapestries
We recommend using a screen six centi-metres thick, made of massive stones, which can be placed anywhere in a room or building to be exposed to cool air streaming in at night through the open windows. Such a screen will then serve to curb the temperature increase in the building during the day.

10 High-emissivity mirror
If the ambient air temperature does not exceed 34°C (the temperature of human skin), a high-emissivity mirror can help cool us off by radiation as our bodies lose heat towards the mirror.

11 High-thermal-effusivity mat
If, once again, the ambient air temperature does not exceed 34°C (the temperature of human skin), a mat made of high-effusivity material (aluminium, copper or stone) laid at the back of a room, far from the windows, will cool us down by conduction upon physical contact, thanks to the rapid transfer of heat from our skin to the mat.

12 Water chimney
To lower the air temperature during a heat wave, we propose a decorative element that

works like a traditional chimney or wood stove, only in reverse—the idea being to cool rather than heat the surrounding air. To this end, we would take advantage of the principle of transpiration: in contact with air, water naturally evaporates. The transition from liquid to gas lowers the air temperature by drawing energy from the air.

13 Cold paint

Since human skin is mostly composed of water, longer wavelengths of electromagnetic radiation warm us up more than shorter wavelengths. Therefore, if walls are painted violet, which has the shortest wavelength in the visible spectrum, they'll cool us down by reflecting the colder wavelengths onto our skin.

Let us conclude with a few last words about the potential health benefits of our novel approach to indoor decoration. Indoor air pollution has been widely documented and discussed in recent years.[74] Formaldehyde, for example, one of the most common volatile organic compounds, has recently been declared a definite carcinogen by the WHO, so plywood, MDF and the like, which contain a lot of formaldehyde in their adhesives, are gradually being replaced by natural wood planks.

A more topical health issue at present is, of course, Covid-19. In November 2015, researchers at the University of Southampton in the UK published a paper comparing how long human coronavirus 229[E] (one of the viruses responsible for the common cold) remains infectious on various

74   See, e.g., the brochure 'Un air sain chez soi' published by the ADEME (French Agency for Environment and Energy): *bitly.ws/Byz8;* or this article by the Swiss Federal Office of Public Health: *bitly.ws/xocM*

materials.[75] They found that this widespread coronavirus was completely inactive after 40 minutes on surfaces of brass (an alloy of copper and zinc) and significantly diminished after 60 minutes on zinc but remained active for more than five days on other metals, as well as on glass and plastic. The more copper a given material contains, the more effective it is at deactivating the virus and preventing transmission between people who touch a contaminated surface one after the other. The experiment was repeated using fingertip simulation to deposit the virus on a copper surface—the way we might contaminate a surface in everyday life—and showed that the virus became harmless within three minutes. What interior designers can glean from these findings is that the brass door handles, knobs and bells of yesteryear actually prevented contamination, and the underlying principles of hygiene might well be worth taking into consideration when choosing materials for architectural and interior design projects.

14 Virucidal handle

Copper is virucidal, so coronaviruses don't survive more than a few minutes on brass, which is an alloy of copper and zinc. This is why we recommend brass for all door handles and handrails.

75 Warnes, Little, Keevil, 2015

It may seem trivial, but simply switching from PVC and stainless steel door handles to brass and from plywood (especially MDF) to raw wood would amount to an aesthetic revolution. For over 70 years, during the so-called postmodern period, in which fossil fuels and antibiotics had by and large rid us of a great many material and health problems, the criteria for choosing architectural materials were solely based on a semantic and analogical decision-making mode: we no longer cared what a material 'is' but what it 'says'.[76] Caught up in a tangled web of cultural references, comparisons and semiotic associations, a given material was regarded merely as a sign, analogy, metaphor or symbol of something else. Its real qualities, its physical, physiological and thermal properties, ceased to be selection criteria. But the Covid-19 pandemic and global warming have turned the situation around and committed us to a new approach to decorative art. The current health and climate crises have put paid to postmodern architecture. We must henceforth choose building materials on the basis not of their semantic or symbolic value but of their physical, biological, chemical and thermal values. We call this aesthetic revolution the Anthropocene style.

76   Rahm, 2020

Catalogue

Low-thermal-effusivity rug

Effusivity

Thermal effusivity is a measure of the rate at which a material exchanges heat with its surroundings.

It depends on an object's conductivity, density and specific heat capacity. Effusivity applies at the contact surface between objects. A material with a high e-value will exchange heat with its surroundings faster. When two objects come into contact, the resulting temperature at the interface depends on each object's temperature and effusivity and will be closer to that of the material with the higher effusivity.

Material	Effusivity $(kJ/[m^2K\sqrt{s}])$
Copper	35
Aluminium	23
Steel	13
Cement	2
Stone	2
Wood	0.4
Human skin	0.4
Cork	0.1
Wool	0.07

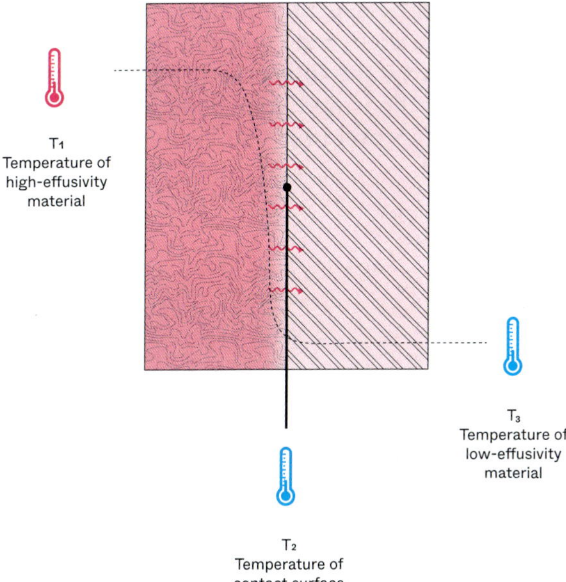

Heat transfer

When a high-effusivity material at a high temperature comes into contact with a low-effusivity material at a low temperature, the temperature at the contact surface will be closer to that of the high-effusivity material.

How it works

When you sit on a cold stone or concrete floor or touch it with your feet, your body loses heat to the floor through direct contact. But that heat transfer can be slowed by placing a material with low effusivity between your body and the floor. Thanks to its low effusivity, the interposed rug will exchange heat with the floor and your body at a very slow rate, thereby protecting you from being cooled by conduction.

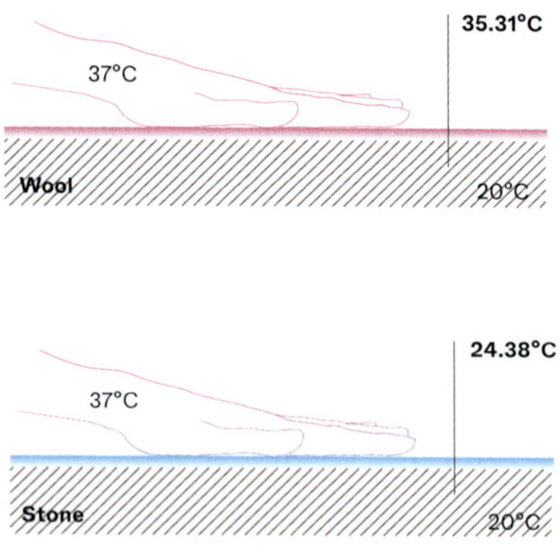

Perceived temperature by material

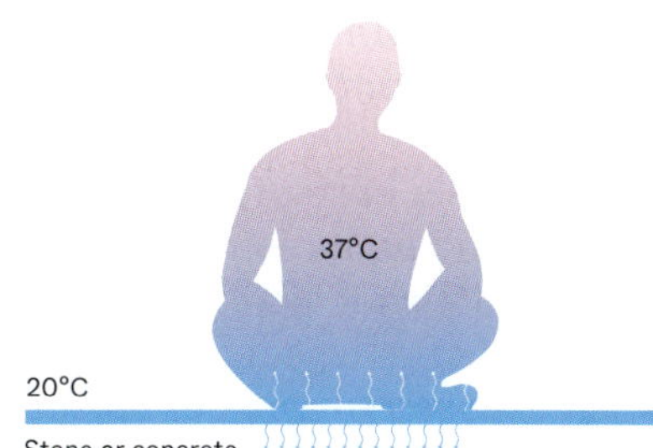

High-emissivity flooring cools the body.

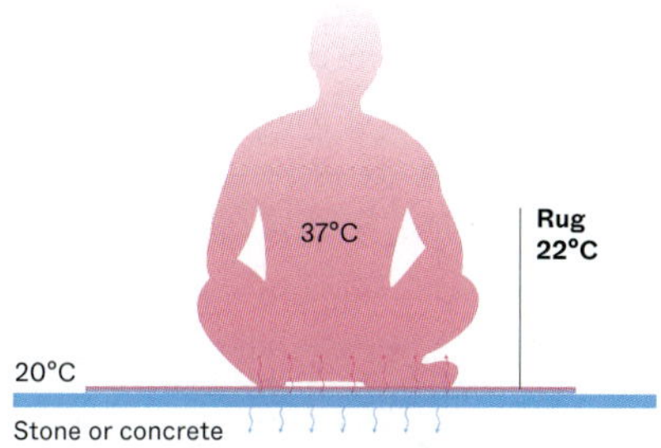

A low-emissivity rug blocks the cold
emanating from the floor.

Low-emissivity curtain

Emissivity
Emissivity is a measure of a material's ability to exchange heat with another material by radiation (without any physical contact).

Thermal emissivity is a measure of how well a given material absorbs and emits infrared radiation and, consequently, how much it increases in temperature when exposed to a hotter object or decreases in temperature when exposed to a colder object—though without any physical contact, solely through the emission of electromagnetic waves through space.

Material	Emissivity (min.= 0; max. = 1)
Copper	0.023–0.052
Aluminium	0.04
Steel	0.43
Cement	0.54
Iron	0.6
Perfect black body	1

Emissivity coefficient
Emissivity ranges from 0 (minimum value) to 1 (maximum value). The lower a material's emissivity, the more infrared it reflects and the less it heats up in the sun. Conversely, the higher a material's emissivity, the more infrared it absorbs and the more it heats up.

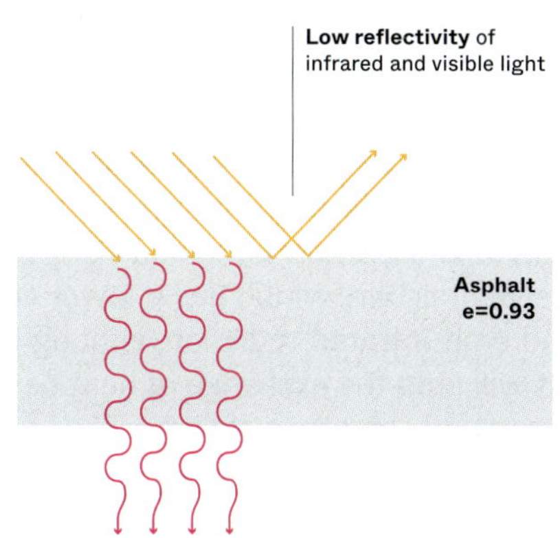

Low reflectivity of infrared and visible light
Asphalt
e=0.93
High level of absorption and emission of heat by radiation

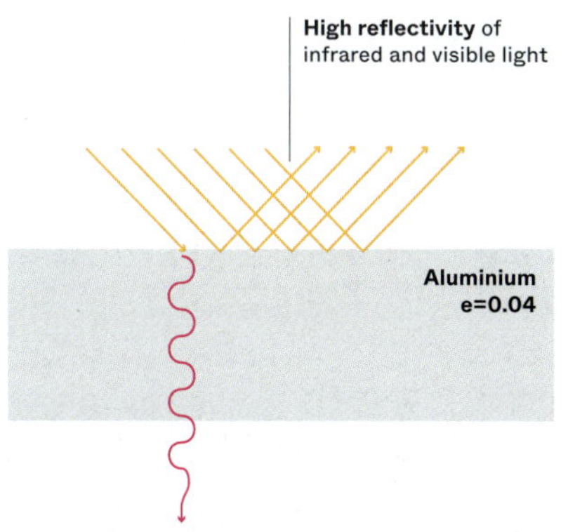

High reflectivity of infrared and visible light
Aluminium
e=0.04
Low level of absorption and emission of heat by radiation

How it works

In the wintertime, if the walls have a high emissivity coefficient, the human body will lose energy—and therefore heat—by infrared radiation to the cold walls. The body's thermal energy is absorbed by the walls and the person is cooled as a result. If a low-emissivity curtain, which has a lower capacity to absorb and emit infrared radiation, is hung in front of the wall, it will stop the exchange of heat between the warm human body and the cold wall. The human body will then not lose heat to the wall.

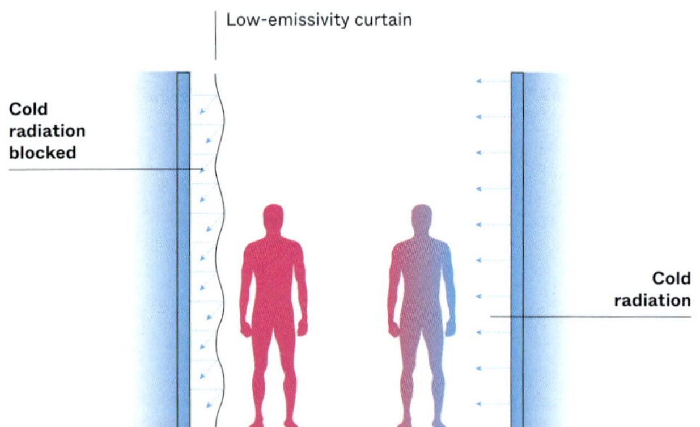

Emissivity and cooling

If the walls are cold and made of a highly emissive material, they will cause the human body to lose heat by infrared radiation (human skin is extremely emissive) and cool down as a result. Conversely, if the walls are made of a low-emissivity material, the body will retain its heat.

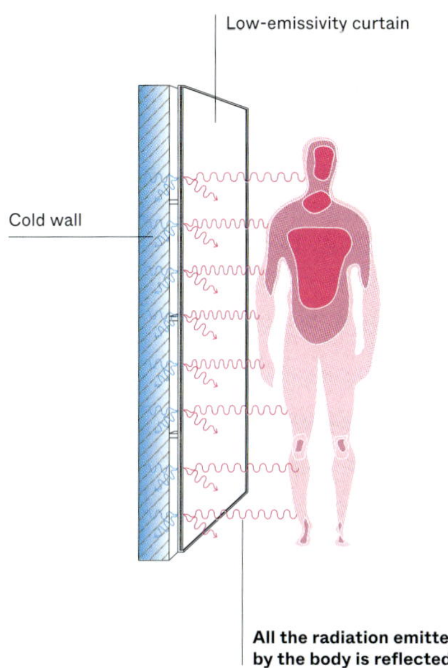

Emissivity and material

The emissivity value depends mainly on the type of material. Metal usually has very low emissivity—i.e., it does not absorb heat from incident radiation. When exposed to the sun, it does not heat up by radiation, but it is brought to the ambient air temperature by convection. Conversely, a material like concrete (e=0.91) or asphalt (e=0.93) heats up in the sun to gradually surpass the ambient air temperature.

High-reflectance mirror

Reflection

Reflection results when the frequency of incident light rays does not match the vibrations of the electrons in the atoms at the surface of a given material.

Energy is reflected because it is not fully absorbed by electrons, which do not vibrate continuously at a large amplitude. There are two basic types of reflection: specular reflection, in which incident energy rays from a single incoming direction are reflected in a single outgoing direction; and diffuse reflection, in which energy from a single incoming direction is scattered at many different angles. These phenomena depend on the wavelength of the radiation and the form and texture of the reflecting surface.

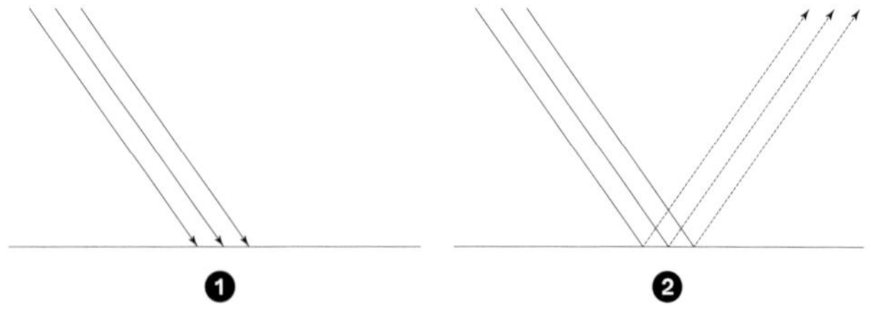

1. Low-reflectance material
2. High-reflectance material

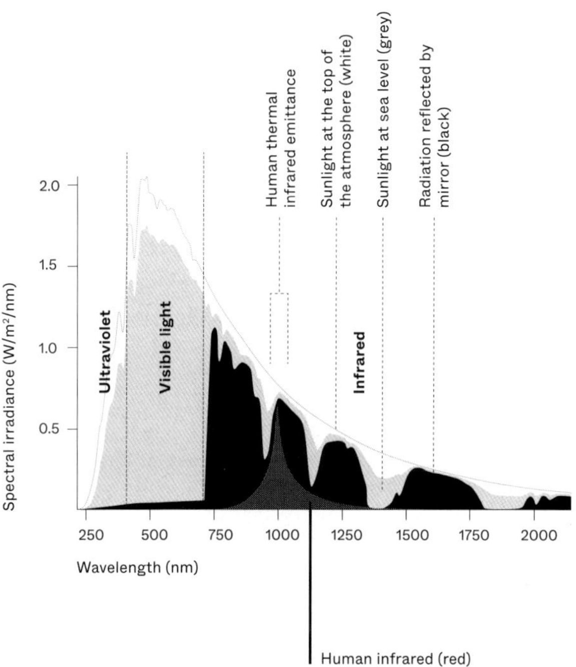

The reflectance spectrum of mirror pigment (shown in black) reflects the invisible human infrared radiation (shown in red), but not visible light.

How it works

Because of its 37°C core temperature and the thermal emissivity of the skin, the human body is always emitting infrared radiation, which is absorbed by the colder surrounding surfaces. Coating a mirror with a layer of material that specifically reflects the infrared wavelengths emitted by the human body back to the emitter will thereby warm up the body.

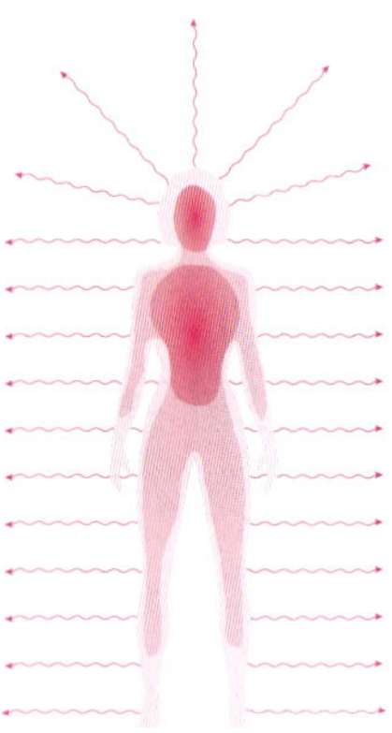

Radiant cooling
The body radiates heat in every direction as a means of regulating its internal temperature. Under normal conditions, this is the most effective means of removing heat.

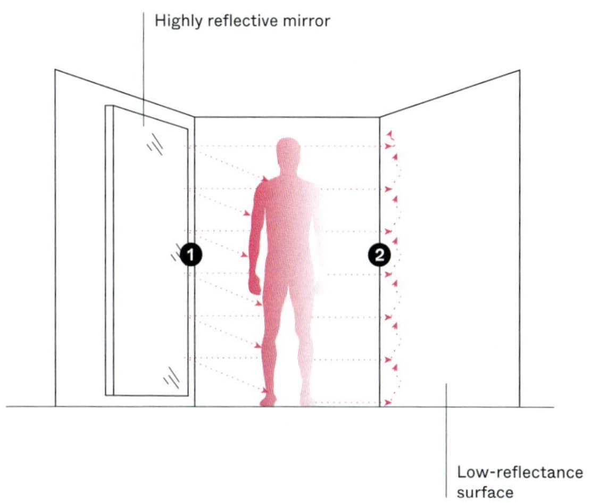

1. The infrared heat emitted by the body is reflected back to it.
2. The infrared heat emitted by the body is absorbed by the wall.

Low-thermal-conductivity tapestry

Conduction

Thermal conduction is the flow of heat through solids and liquids by the combination of vibrations and collisions of molecules and free electrons.

The molecules of a physical system at a higher temperature vibrate faster than those of a system at a lower temperature. This phenomenon occurs without any movement of matter at the contact surface between these systems. Heat continues to flow from a warmer system to a cooler one until they achieve thermal equilibrium—i.e., the same temperature.

Material	Thermal conductivity (k)
Copper	401
Aluminium	205
Steel	43
Concrete	1.7
Oakwood	635
Plasterboard	0.5
Wood	0.17
Rockwool	0.045
Air	0.024

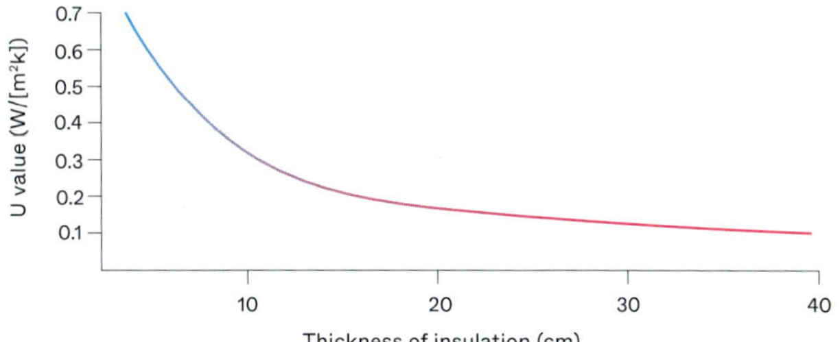

Ideal insulation thickness
The thicker the thermal insulation, the more it will block heat transfers between the inside and outside of a wall. The most effective thickness is 25 cm; beyond 25 cm, the benefit of adding thicker thermal insulation becomes negligible.

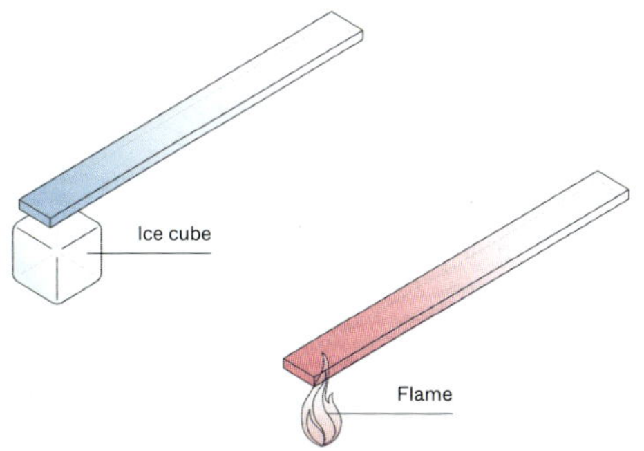

The energy (the coldness of the ice cube or the heat of the flame) flows more or less rapidly through a material according to its thermal conductivity coefficient until uniform thermal equilibrium is reached throughout.

How it works

In a cold climate, the exterior walls of a house are at a lower temperature than the air inside. The layer of indoor air nearest the wall will lose heat by conduction through direct contact, which will in turn lower the temperature of the whole room. By placing a layer of low-conductivity material against the wall, we can prevent conductive heat transfer between the warm indoor air and the cold wall, thereby maintaining a comfortable room temperature.

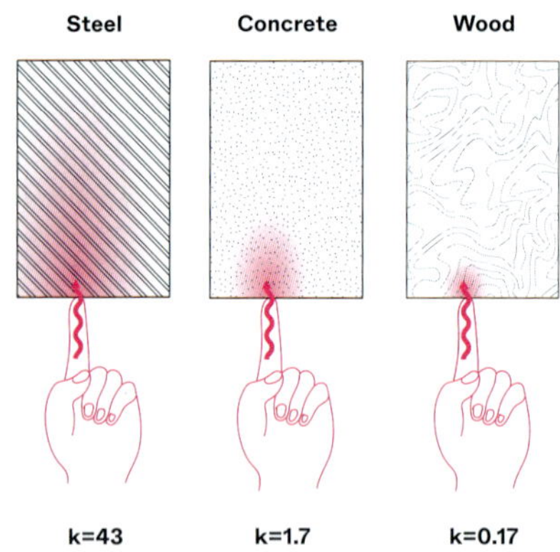

Heat conduction in various materials
The higher a material's k value (heat transfer coefficient in W/[m²K]), the more heat will flow through it. The lower the k value, the better the insulation.

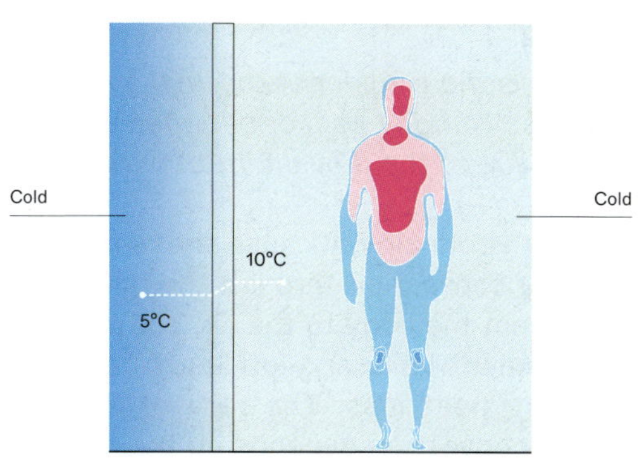

Heat transfer without tapestry

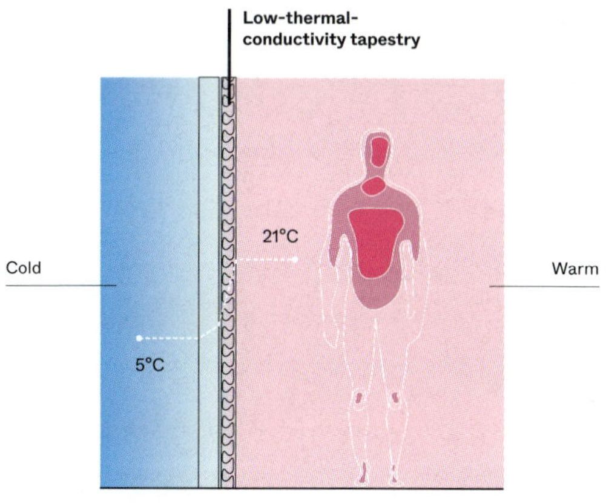

No heat transfer with tapestry

Airtight screen

Convection

Convection is the transfer of thermal energy in a fluid (i.e., liquid or gas) or between a fluid and a solid due to the movement of particles.

Contact with cold air will cause the human body to lose heat by convection through the direct transfer of energy from the body to the air, but also because air in movement will carry off body heat, thereby accelerating heat loss. The rate of heat energy transfer by convection depends on the temperature difference between a fluid and another fluid or a solid and on the existing air movement. As a result, the human body will cool down if the ambient air is colder and if the body is exposed to the wind.

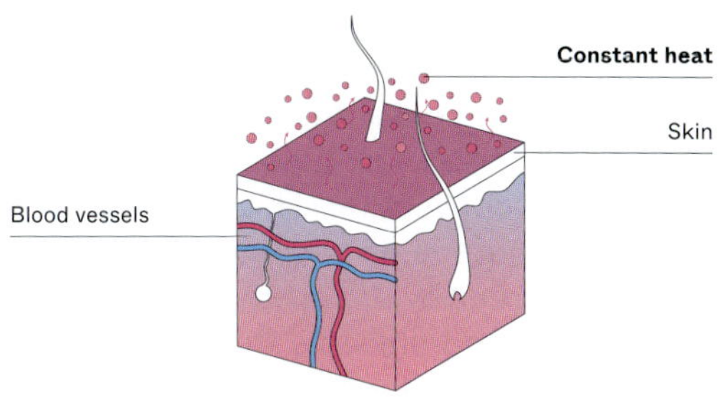

Constant heat on the skin in the absence of wind:
the skin stays warm.

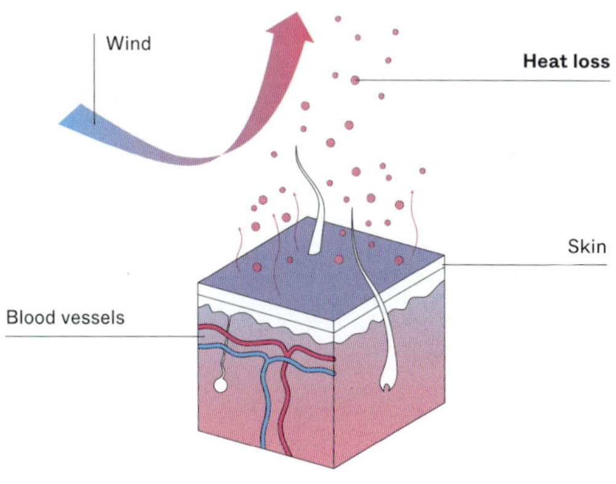

Heat loss caused by contact between skin
and wind: the skin cools off.

How it works

In the absence of air movement, the body always loses heat, which forms a layer of warm air around the skin. When there is air movement, this heat is carried off by the colder moving air, which blows away the film of heat surrounding the body, thereby cooling it by convection. This is why the felt air temperature depends on the wind speed. A head-high airtight screen will stop the movement of air around the body and preserve the layer of warm air, creating a comfortable winter environment even in homes that are less heated.

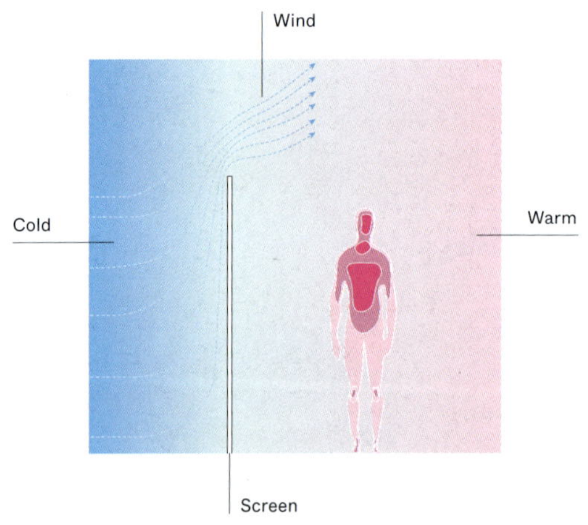

Blocking indoor draughts will keep the body from cooling off through convection, thereby improving thermal comfort in winter.

Low-emissivity mirror

Emissivity

Because the surface material of the mirror has a low emissivity coefficient, it does not absorb or radiate the heat coming from hot air. So a human body in front of this mirror will not receive any thermal radiation from it. If the daytime temperature is high (but below 34°C), the part of the wall covered by the mirror will not radiate heat towards the human body, thus protecting it from overheating.

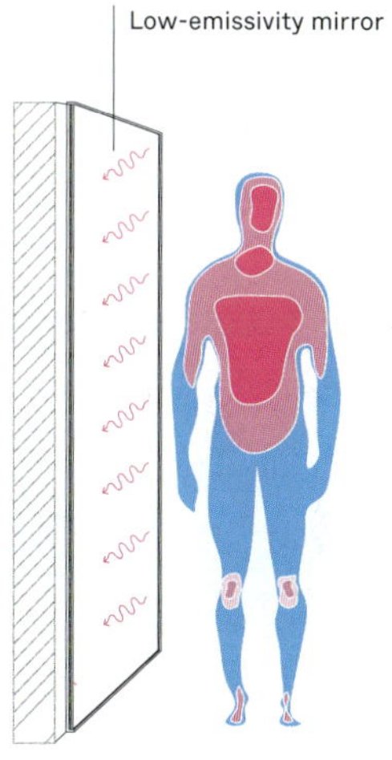

A low-emissivity mirror does not absorb the heat from the outside air, so it keeps a human body facing it cooler.

Convective chair

Convection

When a fluid is warm, its molecules move faster than those of a cold fluid. As a result, the warmer fluid is less dense—i.e., lighter—and moves up towards the ceiling. Archimedes' principle of buoyancy states that a body immersed in a fluid will tend to sink if it is denser than the fluid and, conversely, will tend to rise if it is less dense than the fluid—just as cold air (which is denser) sinks while warm air rises.

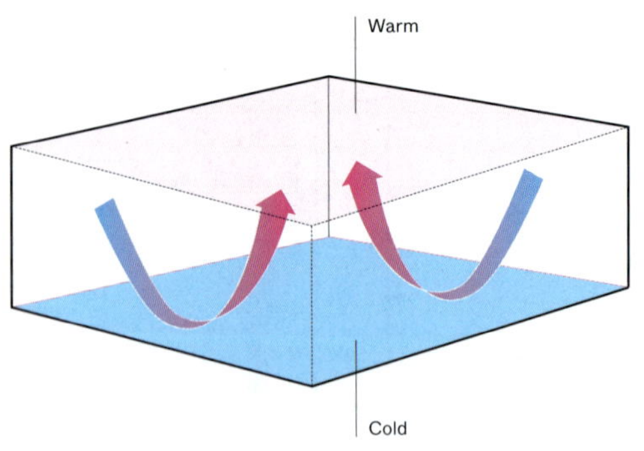

Warm air rises as cold air sinks.

How it works

According to Archimedes' principle, the warm air in a room without much air circulation will accumulate at the ceiling, while the cold air will remain close to the floor. If a chair is raised significantly, the occupant will benefit from the surrounding warmth higher up in the room and enjoy greater thermal comfort in winter. In summer, conversely, we're better off staying closer to the floor, where the human body is surrounded by cooler air.

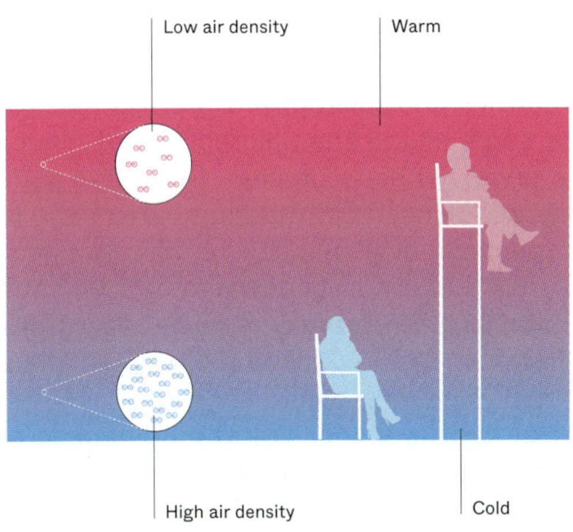

Vertical stratification of heat in the air according to Archimedes' principle of buoyancy.

Spectral-light lamp

Photoreception

When light hits the retina at the back of the eye, it is analysed by the rods and cones of the retina's photoreceptor cells. The human eye contains three kinds of cones, which are most sensitive to wavelengths of 420, 534 and 564 nanometres, respectively, and more active in daylight. The rods' response peaks at a wavelength of 498 nm, and they are more active at night. These light spectra are then sent via the optic nerve to the brain, where they are processed into an image.

A dog's eye contains two kinds of cones, with peak sensitivity at 429 and 555 nm wavelengths, respectively.

Chlorophyll A and chlorophyll B are two types of pigments contained in the chloroplasts of plant cells. In the photosynthesis process, these two pigments absorb wavelengths in the blue part of the visible light spectrum at 410, 430 and 453 nm and in the red part of the visible spectrum at 635, 642 and 662 nm, rejecting the wavelengths between 453 and 635 nm—i.e., in the part of the visible light spectrum that appears green to our eyes.

Spectral light is indoor lighting composed exclusively of wavelengths needed by the inhabitants, so it saves energy and money. First of all, this artificial lighting is made up of semiconductors that emit the precise wavelengths (420, 534, 564 nm) which are actually perceived by the human eye and are important to human health. So spectral light does not waste energy and money on producing wavelengths that are not perceived by the cones in the human eye. But we suggest opening the spectrum up to include the wavelengths that other household inhabitants (dogs, cats, green plants) need to see, grow and photosynthesise. So the spectral-light lamp has twelve semiconductor LEDs, which precisely emit twelve peak wavelengths perceived by humans, dogs and cats, and green plants: 470 nm (blue), 534 nm (green) and 564 nm (yellowish green) for humans; 470 nm (blue) and 555 nm (lime green) for dogs; 500 nm (cyan) and 556 nm (green) for cats; and 470 nm (blue) and 662 nm (deep red) for plants.

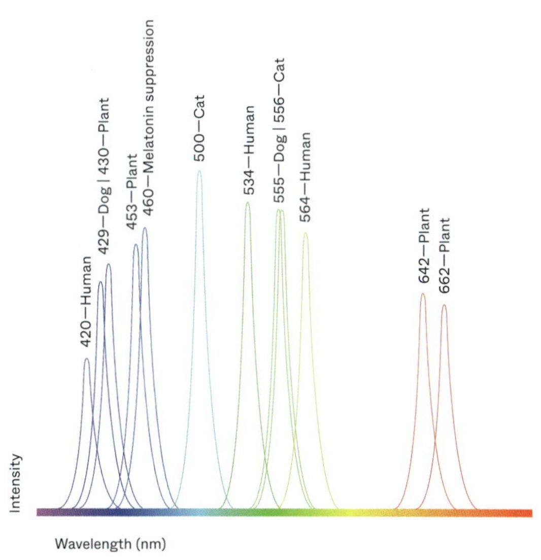

The twelve wavelengths for humans, dogs and cats, and plants

Human

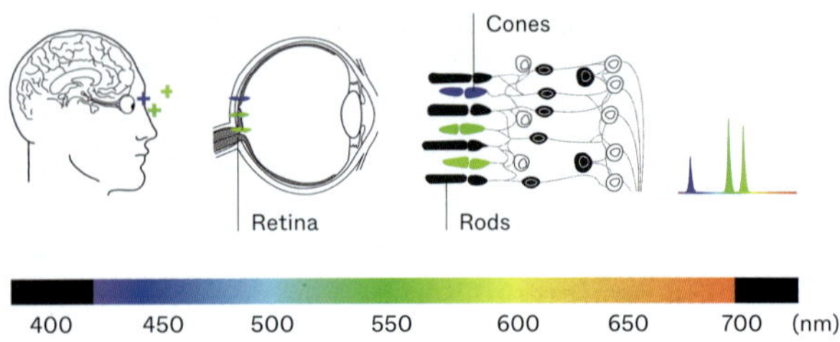

Dog

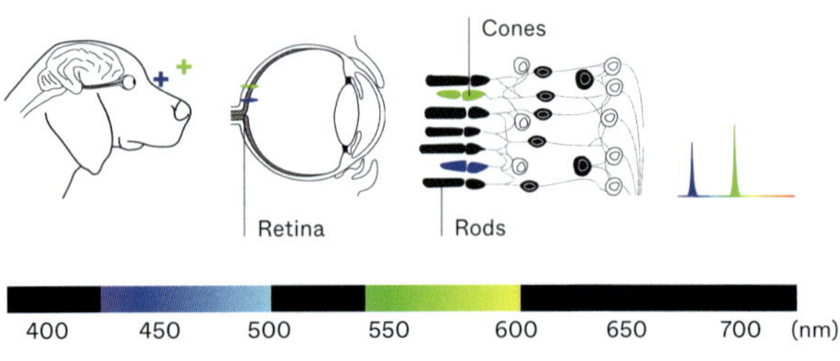

Chlorophyll molecules

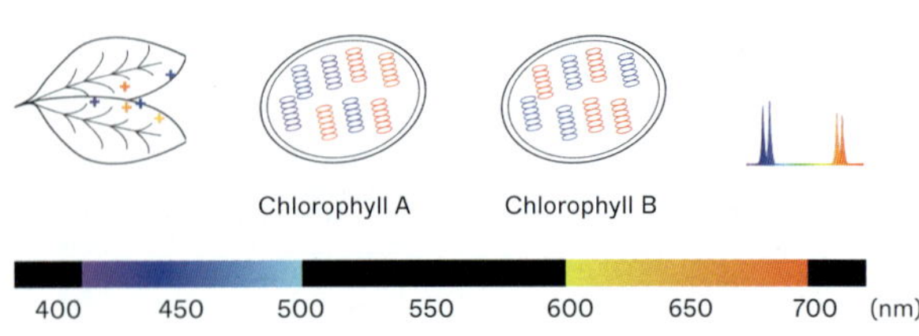

How it works

The concave shape of the upper part of the glass globe directs each of the 36 light tubes towards the opalescent lower surface of the globe, where the twelve rays of different wavelengths converge: their light is mixed and homogenised to produce, by additive colour synthesis, a white-light spectrum like that of natural sunlight.

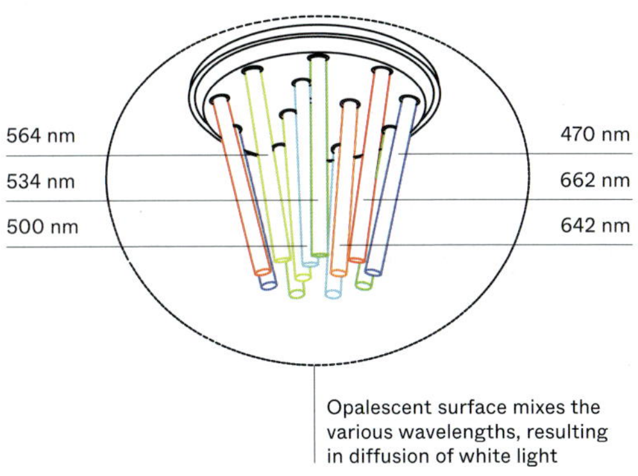

The addition of the various wavelengths that are emitted by the LEDs and perceived by humans, animals and plants yields white light.

Cold paint

Spectral thermal absorption

Water reacts differently according to the wavelength of the light that reaches it. The longer the wavelength (i.e., closer to the infrared band of the electromagnetic spectrum), the more energy the water gains and the more it heats up as a result. Conversely, the shorter the wavelength of incident light reaching the water (closer to ultraviolet), the less energy the water gains, so it remains cold under the light. Water absorbs 100 times more energy from red light than from blue light—and reacts even less to violet light.

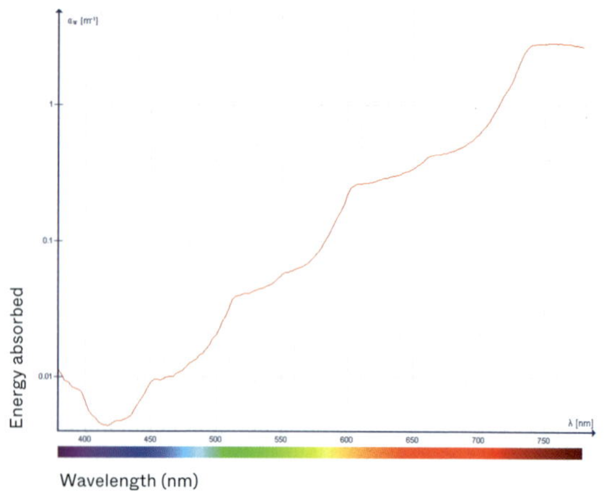

Energy gained by water due to
wavelength of incident light

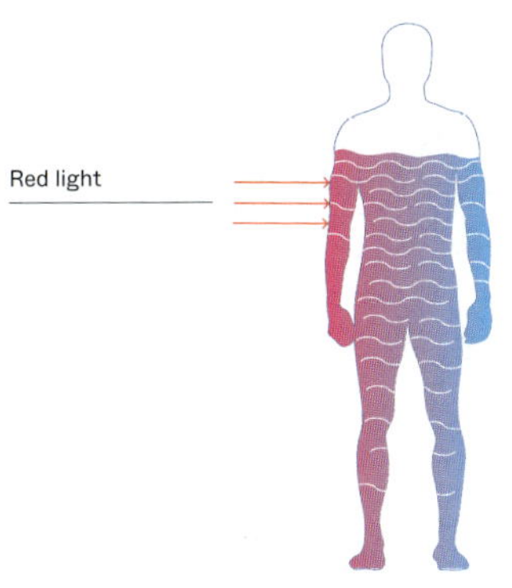

Red light warms up the human body.

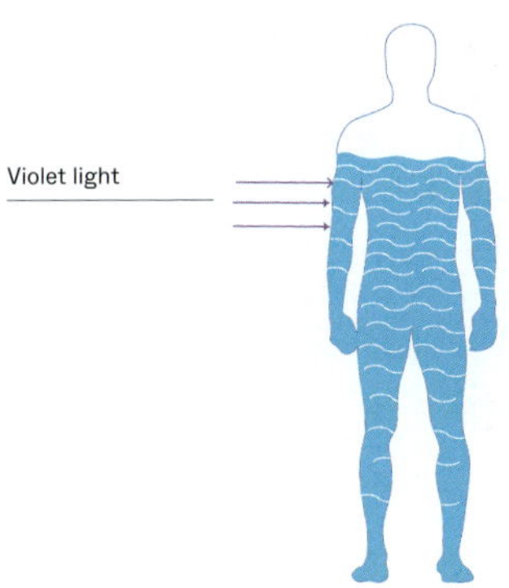

Violet light does not warm up the body.

How it works

The wall is painted violet so it will reflect only violet, the wavelength which is least absorbed by water and which consequently heats up water the least. Since the human body is chiefly composed of water, it does not warm up upon receiving violet light by radiation.

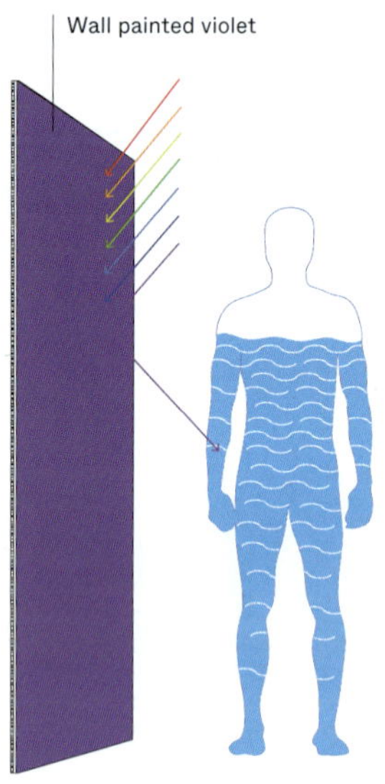

Physiological and climate criteria determine this aesthetic choice.

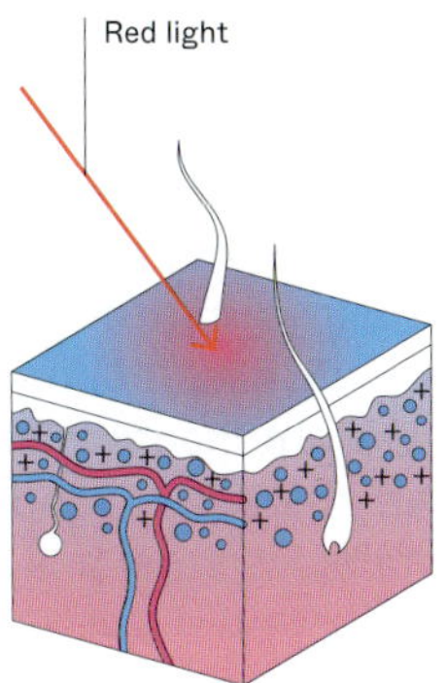

Red light warms up human skin.

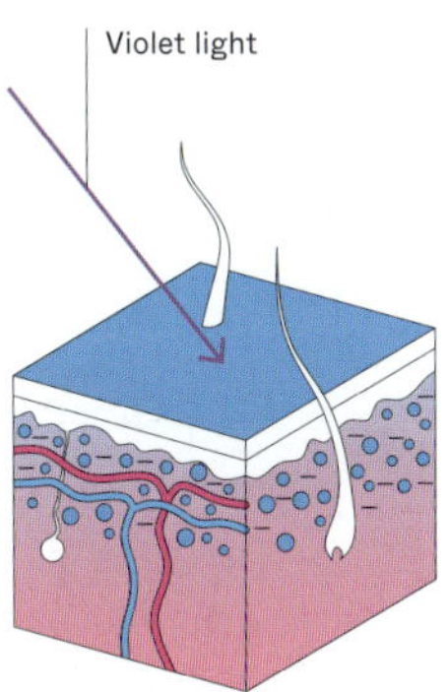

Violet light does not warm up human skin.

Virucidal door handle

Antiviral properties

Copper (Cu) and its alloys have excellent anti-viral and antimicrobial properties. Recent studies show that these alloys can effectively inactivate the Covid-19 virus. Viruses deposited by the hand on a copper surface are inactivated within minutes, whereas they remain active and contagious for several days on stainless steel and on plastic.

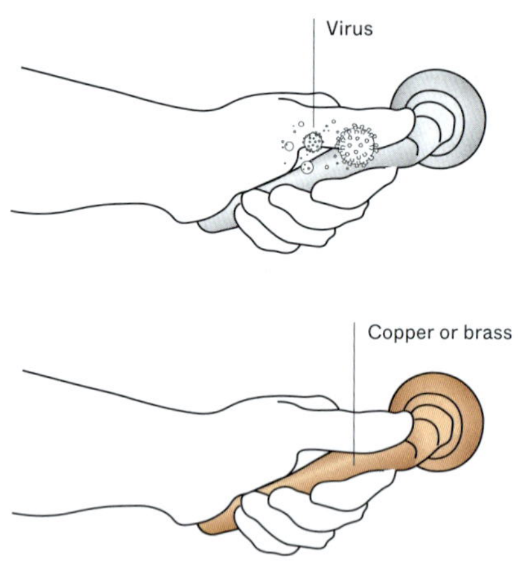

Door handles and handrails made of copper or brass serve to ward off contamination.

Philippe Rahm was born in 1967 in Pully, Switzerland, studied architecture at the EPFL (Swiss Federal Institute of Technology in Lausanne) and did his PhD in architecture at the University of Paris-Saclay in 2019. He set up his own firm in Paris in 2008 and has since garnered an international reputation for sustainable architecture. Among other things, he designed the Climatorium in Taichung, Taiwan, which opened in 2020, and, together with OMA, won first prize for a master plan to redevelop Farini, a 62-hectare urban district in Milan. Rahm has taught at Princeton, Harvard, Columbia and Cornell and is now an associate professor at HEAD, the Geneva University of Art and Design. He has exhibited at the biennials in Venice (2002, 2008), Sharjah, United Arab Emirates (2019) and Tallinn (2022). His latest published books are *Le jardin météorologique* (2019) and *Écrits climatiques* (2020, both published by Éditions B2), *Météorologie des sentiments* (2020, Les Petits Matins) and *Histoire naturelle de l'architecture* (2020, Pavillon de l'Arsenal).

Thermal efficiency standards and regulations for buildings in Switzerland, France and Germany

Switzerland

Minergie, Swiss nationwide label: www.minergie.ch

Energy efficiency legislation, Canton of Vaud:
www.vd.ch/themes/environnement/energie/legislation/

www.vd.ch/themes/environnement/energie/legislation/reglement-sur-le-cecb/

France

Règles Th-bat (rules for calculating the energy performance of buildings): Opaque partitions (20 Dec. 2017):
www.rt-batiment.fr/documents/rt2012/thbat/4-Fascicule_parois_opaques_methodes.pdf

Decree No. 2017-919 of 9 May 2017, to amend articles R. 131-28-7 and R. 131-28-9 of the Building and Housing Code:
www.legifrance.gouv.fr/jorf/id/JORFTEXT000034639364

Thermal regulation RT 2012:
www.ecologie.gouv.fr/reglementation-thermique-rt2012

Environmental regulation RE 2020: www.rt-batiment.fr/IMG/pdf/guide_re2020_dhup-cerema.pdf

Germany

Passivhaus : www.passiv.de

References

Alexandre, A., *Histoire de l'art décoratif du XVIe siècle à nos jours*, Paris, Librairie Renouard, 1892

Banham, R., *The Architecture of Well-Tempered Environment*, London, Architectural Press, 1969

Besset, M., *Le Corbusier*, Geneva, Skira, 1968

Cardon, É., *L'art au foyer domestique (la décoration de l'appartement)*, Paris, Librairie Renouard, 1884

Crutzen, P.J., Stoermer, E.F., 'The "Anthropocene"', *Global Change,* Newsletter No. 41, International Geosphere-Biosphere Programme (IGBP), May 2000

Duvette, C., Volle H., Walter, M., *Intérieurs parisiens*, Paris, Parigramme, 2016

Giedion, S., *Mechanization Takes Command*, Minneapolis, University of Minnesota Press, [1948] 2014

Havard, H., *L'art dans la maison (grammaire de l'ameublement)*, Paris, Rouveyre et G. Blond, 1884

Havard, H., *Les arts de l'ameublement. La décoration*, Paris, Charles Delagraves, 1897

Jandot, O., *Les Délices du feu. L'homme, le chaud et le froid à l'époque moderne*, Paris, Champ Vallon, 2017

Le Corbusier, *L'Art décoratif d'aujourd'hui*, Paris, Crès, 1925

Le Corbusier, *Vers une architecture*, Paris, Flammarion, [1923] 2008

Loos, A., *Ornement et Crime*, Paris, Rivages, [1913] 2015

Morris, I., *Foragers, Farmers, and Fossil Fuels : How Human Values Evolve*, Princeton, Princeton University Press, 2017

Neumeyer, F., *Mies van der Rohe. Réflexions sur l'art de bâtir*, Paris, Le Moniteur, 1996

Rahm, P., 'Comment l'isolation par l'extérieur est-elle en train de révolutionner l'architecture', in *Be.Passive,* No. 12, 2012, www.issuu.com/bepassive/docs/bepassive12fr

Rahm, P., 'Coronavirus ou le retour à la normale', in *AOC,* 2020, www.aoc.media/opinion/2020/03/09/coronavirus-ou-le-retour-a-la-normale/

Rahm, P., *Histoire naturelle de l'architecture*, Paris, Pavillon de l'Arsenal, 2020,

Rahm, P., Nguyen, P. (eds.), *Architecture du nouveau réalisme,* Madrid, Asimetricas, 2020,

Rahm, P., Nguyen, P. (eds.), *Decorative Arts in the Age of Global Warming,* Madrid, Asimetricas, 2021,

Röck, M., et al., 'Embodied GHG Emissions of Buildings —the Hidden Challenge for Effective Climate Change Mitigation', in *Applied Energy,* No. 258, 2020

Semper, G., *Du style et de l'architecture: Écrits, 1834-1869,* Paris, Parenthèses, 2007

Soulillou, J., 'Y a-t-il lieu de parler du décoratif ?', in *Chimères. Revue des schizoanalyses,* No. 17, fall 1992

Viel-Castel, H. (comte de), *Exposition des beaux-arts appliqués à l'industrie, tapis et tapisserie,* Paris, *Journal des Demoiselles,* April 1864

Warnes, S.L., Little, Z.R., Keevil, C.W., 'Human Coronavirus 229[E] Remains Infectious on Common Touch Surface Materials', *mBio,* 6(6):e01697-15, 2015

Welzer, H., *Les guerres du climat. Pourquoi on tue au XXIe siècle,* Paris, Gallimard, 2009

HEAD–Publishing, 2023

Texts licensed under
CC BY–SA

Title: The Anthropocene Style

Original title:
Le style anthropocène

Author: Philippe Rahm

Manifestes collection edited
by Julie Enckell Julliard and
Anthony Masure

Editorial coordinator:
Sylvain Menétrey

Scientific proofreader:
Javier Fernández Contreras

Translator: Eric Rosencrantz

Proofreader:
Juliana Froggatt

Graphic charter:
Dimitri Broquard

Graphic design:
Alicia Dubuis

Fonts:
ABC Whyte (Dinamo, 2019),
Lyon Text (Commercial Type,
2009)

Printed by Imprimerie Prestige
Graphique, Plan-les-Ouates

ISBN: 978-2-940510-79-5

Legal deposit: April 2023

Hes·so

**—HEAD
Genève**

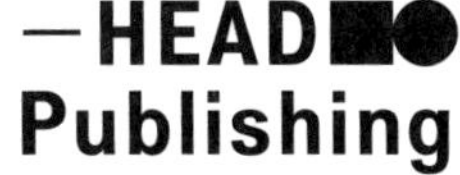

—HEAD
Publishing